Supporting Boys' Writing in the Early Years

How do we give young children a writer's voice and allow them to become creative and inspired writers?

Supporting Boys' Writing in the Early Years shows you how you can help boys to become confident and capable writers by supporting them to write in ways that make sense to them – on the move, outside and inside, in dens, in bushes, in mud or sprawled on the floor dressed as superheroes. Drawing on four boys' writing projects involving over 80 practitioners, the book reveals that a playful, child-centred approach can allow boys *and* girls to develop a writer's voice and raise attainment in writing as well as enhancing all aspects of young children's development.

With a strong focus on observation-led assessment and planning, the book is full of practical ideas to improve the writing environment and provide writing opportunities that will be enjoyable and motivating for children. Featuring a wide range of case studies, the book covers:

- the stages that children move through in learning to write;
- how you can change and develop your learning environments to give children inspiring resources and opportunities to write;
- helping children to find a purpose to write through their play;
- practical ways to create a partnership with parents that builds on their strengths as educators at home.

This book will help you to create a truly enabling environment for writing and is essential reading for all those that want the children in their setting to become confident, motivated and creative writers.

Julie Cigman is an Early Years teacher, trainer and consultant. She runs courses and workshops on early writing and supporting boys' learning in the EYFS.

'Julie Cigman's book uses a vast range of personal vignettes to explain best practice when encouraging boys to write. The theory is brought to life with these recollections, making this a very informative and enjoyable book to read. The circumstances described in the Chapter "Finding a Voice" really resonated, where the boys who are difficult to engage are described with expert insight. The ideas for working together with boys are beautifully simple and are tried and tested. This book would support both experienced practitioners and those who are just starting out, because it is so accessible and uses examples in such a delightful way.'

– **Kathy Brodie**, Author of *Observation, Assessment and Planning in the Early Years*

'Julie Cigman has given us a practical and principled way forward in supporting boys' writing. This book is shot through with rich examples of effective practice and deserves to be widely used. Building on sound educational foundations, the suggestions and discussions help committed teachers and practitioners enhance young boys' literacy development. Young boys' writing is bought alive for us in these pages, and the groundedness in practice demonstrates how boys' achievement in writing can be appropriately supported from an early age. This is a book for everyone interested in promoting early literacy development. An excellent read and a practical compendium.'

– **Professor Cathy Nutbrown**, *School of Education, The University of Sheffield*

Supporting Boys' Writing in the Early Years

Becoming a writer in leaps and bounds

Julie Cigman

Routledge
Taylor & Francis Group
LONDON AND NEW YORK

First published 2014
by Routledge
2 Park Square, Milton Park, Abingdon, Oxon OX14 4RN

and by Routledge
711 Third Avenue, New York, NY 10017

Routledge is an imprint of the Taylor & Francis Group, an informa business

© 2014 Julie Cigman

The right of Julie Cigman to be identified as author of this work has been asserted by her in accordance with sections 77 and 78 of the Copyright, Designs and Patents Act 1988.

All rights reserved. No part of this book may be reprinted or reproduced or utilised in any form or by any electronic, mechanical, or other means, now known or hereafter invented, including photocopying and recording, or in any information storage or retrieval system, without permission in writing from the publishers.

Trademark notice: Product or corporate names may be trademarks or registered trademarks, and are used only for identification and explanation without intent to infringe.

British Library Cataloguing in Publication Data
A catalogue record for this book is available from the British Library

Library of Congress Cataloging in Publication Data
Supporting boys' writing in the early years : becoming a writer in leaps and bounds / Julie Cigman.
    pages cm
    1. English language–Composition and exercises–Study and teaching (Elementary) 2. Boys–Education (Elementary) I. Title.
    LB1576.C5569 2014
    372.62'3–dc23   2013047750

ISBN: 978-0-415-82610-5 (hbk)
ISBN: 978-0-415-82611-2 (pbk)
ISBN: 978-1-315-77218-9 (ebk)

Typeset in Zapf Humanist
by Keystroke, Station Road, Codsall, Wolverhampton

Printed and bound by CPI Group (UK) Ltd, Croydon, CR0 4YY

This book is dedicated to Rachel and Simon,
who taught me about infinite possibilities.

Contents

List of figures ix
Foreword xi
Acknowledgements xv
Introduction xix

1	Write from the start	1
2	Creating a writing-rich environment	18
3	Discovering a writer's voice	36
4	Writing for a purpose	55
5	The role of the adult in supporting young writers	74
6	Writing and cross-curricular learning	93
7	Working with parents to support early writing	112
8	Conclusion	125

Appendix 1 Boys' Writing Project – the action planning process   131
Appendix 2 Boys' Writing Project play audit   133
Appendix 3 Boys' Writing Project case study   139
Appendix 4 Boys' Writing Project – end of project summary   140
References and further reading   142

Index   147

Figures

1.1 Example 1: Independent mark making by Vincenzo, aged 3, in his play — 5
1.2 Example 2: Independent writing by a 3-year-old girl, Aalia, following a group session when the adult modelled writing a letter to Barty Bear — 6
1.3 Example 3: Independent writing by Cayley, aged 4 years. She has written a letter: *D M* (Dear Mum), *W Y E K T G* (Would you like (to) come to Grandpont) – which she has put in an envelope and written *J M* (Julie's Mum) — 6
1.4 Example 4: Independent writing by Arlo, aged 4 *Wus pon tum* (Once upon a time) *Livt L Fri bes* (lived the three bears) *bEbE bAEy mumE* (baby bear mummy) — 7
1.5 Example 5: Diary written by Simon, aged 5 — 8
1.6 A child is writing with his teacher outside — 10
1.7 Servants — 12
1.8 Princesses — 13
2.1 Develop a 'catch me writing' culture and display photos of the children mark making or writing with scribed captions — 27
2.2 Noah is drawing a dragon as part of his play — 30
3.1 Three boys are playing 'Winter Olympics' — 41
3.2 Children enjoy writing about things that they can do well — 45
4.1 Children labelled their self-portraits — 61
4.2 Sam's writing took off when he started adding speech bubbles to his drawings — 65
4.3 Children developed complex stories based on their model making — 66
5.1 Making posters for the classroom — 80

Figures

5.2 George made a sign as part of his play	85
5.3 Writing labels	87
6.1 Children found their names for the self-registration board	99
6.2 Writing belts encouraged children to write in their play	103
6.3 A classroom display shows how a group of children made an animated film	107
6.4 Casey's model	109
7.1 A 'talking album'	117

Foreword

Many years ago, I was a primary headteacher, my own teaching experience all in Key Stage 2. One day a fellow head (who had always taught in Key Stage 1) made this controversial statement in a teachers' meeting: 'I don't think we should make children write stories till they're at least eight.'

Her remark appalled me. I'd been the sort of little girl who delighted in scribbling stories from the moment she could pick up a pencil, and if anyone had made me wait till I was eight, I'd have gone mad. It took 30 years and a visit to Finland to help me realize I'd been guilty of selective listening. 'I don't think we should *make* children write stories' is very different from 'I don't think we should *let* children write stories'.

Since then, I've written a couple of books myself about writing in the Early Years, one of them with the remarkable Early Years specialist Ros Bayley, and I'd now heartily endorse what that KS1 headteacher said. If it were up to me, schools wouldn't *make* children do any creative writing till they were developmentally equipped to rally the vast range of language and literacy skills that underpin the writing process – and, for some children, that may well not be until they're about eight.

However, if their early literacy experiences are based on the sort of practice described in Julie Cigman's delightful book, I'm sure the overwhelming majority would be champing at the bit to write stories far sooner than that. Children with something exciting to record, and adult helpers who show genuine interest in their ideas, are usually desperate to put pencil to paper, or crayon to clipboard, or chalk to pavement.

The very first thing I saw in a Finnish kindergarten was a group of six-year-old boys who'd arrived early for the morning session and were intently engaged at the writing table. 'They're *boys*,' I gibbered in amazement, 'sitting round a table writing . . . voluntarily!' The Finnish teacher gave me a quizzical look. 'Yes,' she said, 'They like to write.'

The reason boys like to write in Finland is that nobody forces them to do it. Instead, practitioners orchestrate the sort of exciting experiences Julie describes here, then when children are keen to record their ideas, they offer support appropriate to each individual. So young writers of both sexes develop their skills naturally, because it's fun.

Of course, the Finnish kindergarten stage is much longer than our Foundation Phase – it lasts from three to seven – and there are no national profiling exercises or tests to distract practitioners from encouraging children to learn through play. It pays off too – Finland regularly has the best literacy results in Europe, as well as a high level of childhood wellbeing and one of the smallest gaps between rich and poor in the world. They also have a far smaller gap in achievement between boys and girls than here in the UK, where we are rapidly dropping down the international literacy charts, have a shamefully low level of childhood wellbeing and the biggest gap between rich and poor in Europe.

Mind you, despite the demands of our Foundation Stage Profile and the Year 1 and 2 tests, practitioners in England (and the rest of the UK, where there may be fewer tests but practice is still distorted by our national obsession with targets) *can* take a developmentally appropriate approach to writing. All you have to do is follow Julie Cigman's wise advice in this book. Like the practitioners in her research study, you'll find that your children will soon be motivated to explore and express their understanding through writing. You'll also have much more fun than practitioners who merely coax, cajole and coerce their pupils to perform adult-directed tasks that have no real meaning for them.

Indeed – if you can manage to forget about targets and concentrate on *real* Early Years education – I'm pretty certain that, in most cases, your children will achieve the targets too. Even if they don't they'll have a firm foundation for future literacy learning . . . and learning in general.

Although Julie's project was inspired by the need to narrow the gap in literacy achievement between boys and girls, the type of practice she advocates is just as important for ensuring girls' all-round development. The UK's notoriously early start to formal education has generally advantaged girls in terms of profile and test performances, but I believe there have been unintended consequences. For many decades now girls have been learning at a very early age that 'doing what teacher says' results in plenty of ticks and praise: they swiftly become compliant. Perhaps that's one of the reasons that our overwhelmingly female profession has allowed the present tick-box mentality to flourish.

So it's definitely time, for the sake of the next generation, to be brave! Let Julie Cigman show you how the power of play – backed up by the exercise of professional judgement – will help your children become writers by leaps and bounds. And then . . . ENJOY!

– Sue Palmer, Author of *Foundations of Literacy* and *Toxic Childhood: How the Modern World Is Damaging Our Children . . . and What We Can Do about It.*

Acknowledgements

I would like to give first and greatest thanks to all of the children and practitioners who took part in the boys' writing projects between 2009 and 2012. They shared their enthusiasm, their imaginative ideas and their experiences so generously and it is these experiences that have allowed the book to come into being.

The projects grew out of the vision of Elizabeth Fee, and my thanks to Gloucestershire County Council and Oxfordshire County Council who recognized the vision and provided practical and financial support to allow the projects to happen.

Cathy Nutbrown, Peter Hannon and the M.Ed. team at the University of Sheffield gave me the initial inspiration to research and expand my knowledge and understanding of how young children become literate in a developmentally appropriate way, for which a huge thanks, as this determined my path for the following years. Thanks to all the staff and families at Bartlemas Nursery School in Oxford, in particular Carolyn Booth and Nick Swarbrick, who gave me their trust and the scope to try out new ideas for promoting young children's writing.

Julie Fisher provided deeply principled guidance and leadership during my years as an advisory teacher in Oxfordshire, when I learnt so much about how young children develop and learn. Thank you, Julie, for being a guiding light.

I spent many fascinating hours with colleagues and friends, Pat Greenhalf, Amanda Bruce, Sue Hale and Teresa Broad debating the reality of gender differences, nature versus nurture and sharing our observations and experiences regarding boys' preferences and learning styles and needs. I worked alongside many other stimulating and committed colleagues, too many to

Acknowledgements

name everyone individually, but thank you all. To Anni McTavish, who has recently become a much-valued colleague, thank you for all your support.

My profound thanks go to my dearest friend Christine Christiansen who encouraged and cajoled me through all the ups and downs I experienced as I wrote this book. She continued to keep faith in me until the very last stages of her illness and I miss her more than words can say.

Thank you to my parents for my childhood, full of books, storytelling, songs and imaginative play. My childhood memories are very close to many of the playful experiences that you can read about in this book.

My children, Rachel and Simon, provided inspiration as well as support – Simon as a wonderfully creative early writer, Rachel as a wonderfully creative child and adult writer. My grandchildren's voices come through in this book as they too showed their creativity and imagination as children do, in their play.

Thank you to Annamarie Kino and Pardy Dhillon of David Fulton, who gave me encouraging and sensitive advice and support throughout the writing process, for which I am immensely grateful.

To Martin, immense thanks and love for reading and responding to all stages of my writing, when I needed a reader 'Now, this minute!' His responses have always been wise and full of incite and he has been an invaluable support and provider of emotional strength throughout my journey.

I would also like to thank the following schools:

Gloucestershire schools and settings

Abbeydale Playgroup
Abbeymead Primary School
   Abbeymead Under 5s
Foxmoor Primary School
Hempsted Playgroup
Hempsted Primary
Hopebrook Primary
Innsworth Infant School
Larkfield Playgroup
Little Foxes Nursery School
Longhope Playgroup
Mickleton Playgroup

Mickleton Primary School
Mickleton School Nursery
Nailsworth C of E Primary School
Nibley House Nursery
North Nibley C of E Primary School
North Nibley Playgroup
Phoenix Playmates
Pippins Preschool
Stone with Woodford C of E Primary
Stone with Woodford Playgroup

Oxfordshire schools and settings

All Saints C of E Primary School
Bayards Hill Primary School
Bloxham Pre-School
Bloxham Primary School
Chalgrove Primary School
Church Cowley St James Primary School
Drayton Pre-school
Drayton Primary School
East Oxford Primary School
Edith Moorhouse Primary School
Edward Fields Primary School
Glory Farm Primary School
Grove Primary School
Hanborough Manor Primary School
Harwell Primary School
Horspath Primary School
Little Pippins
Long Hanborough Playgroup
Long Hanborough Pre-school
Longworth Pre-School
Mortimer Hall Pre-school, Oxford
Northbourne Pre-School
Northbourne Primary School
Queens Dyke Primary School

Acknowledgements

Rosehill Primary School
Southwold Primary School
Stanford in the Vale Pre-school
Stanford in the Vale Primary School
Stephen Freeman Primary School
St John Fisher Primary School, Oxford
St Nicholas Primary School, Oxford
The John Henry Newman Primary School
West Kidlington Primary School
William Fletcher Primary School
Willowcroft Primary School
Wood Farm Primary School

> *I will remember that I do not teach a curriculum, a concept or an idea, I teach a human being, whose learning is linked to and affected by their community and experience, and that learning in our classroom may affect the student's family, economic future and connection to society.*
>
> Derek Keenan's Hippocratic oath for education 2011
> http://www.mrkeenan.com/?p=595

Introduction

Supporting Boys' Writing in the Early Years has had a long gestation period. The book was conceived in 2008 after Gloucestershire's Early Years adviser, Elizabeth Fee, asked me to devise a boys' writing project with ten Reception classes and their feeder pre-schools. The aim was to 'narrow the gap' between the achievement of boys and girls in writing as measured by the standardized assessment at the end of the Foundation Stage. The project was designed with social constructivist learning theories and a belief in the power of play in its DNA and it contained the potential for real change as practitioners and children worked together to create powerful learning environments. Young children were recognized as instinctive learners, 'inventing and reinventing themselves as thinking people before the world tells them what to think' (Gussin Paley, 2008), and, through the project, practitioners helped children to learn the writing skills needed to develop their potential as 'thinking people'.

The project lead practitioners – Reception and Year 1 teachers, nursery nurses, learning support assistants, pre-school supervisors and pre-school practitioners – worked with their colleagues to develop their setting's practice and provision for early writing. They went far beyond simply introducing some new ideas and resources. At the start of the projects, practitioners discovered that many of the children, especially the boys, were being given limited opportunities to express their natural exuberance and creativity. Their drive to ask questions and explore their world was being valued less than the ability to absorb teacher-directed learning. Conformity was prioritized over inventiveness. Practitioners recognized that children establish beliefs about their abilities as learners from a very young age, picking up messages from adults, both positive and negative, about the type of learning that is valued and the types of things they are expected to do and allowed to do.

Introduction

So, during the projects, practitioners used their observations to move from a focus on boys' 'symptoms', such as *'noisy'*, *'can't sit still'*, *'fidgety'*, *'finds it difficult to concentrate'* to a focus on boys' stories: *'he loves climbing trees'*, *'he loves to be involved in things'*, *'he prefers to kneel or lie down when he writes'*, *'he likes being given special responsibility'*. The boys' stories were used as a starting point for positive interventions that proved to be transformational for settings and for practitioners' understanding of their children.

The first project in Gloucestershire was such a success that Oxfordshire's Early Years team funded a further three projects. Funding was targeted at improving the writing attainment of boys, as they fell behind girls according to scores in the Early Years Foundation Stage Profile. However, the lessons that we all learnt – the practitioners and myself as the consultant who designed and supported the projects – were relevant for *all* children and for all areas of learning.

It's all about good Early Years practice!

Who is this book for?

Supporting Boys' Writing in the Early Years has been written for practitioners working within the EYFS, teacher trainers and university lecturers, students and parents of young children. It shares the voices, experiences and enthusiasm of more than 80 practitioners and the children in their settings as they worked together to create a learning environment where young boys could become writers. The book is for anyone who wants to help children to become writers in the way they learn best – actively, in 'leaps and bounds'.

It provides a simple framework, supported by up-to-date research, that can be followed by anyone who would like to undertake a simple action research project and is supported by some of the documentation that was used during the projects in the appendices.

Each chapter covers one aspect of the journey undertaken during the project and has examples of developing practice that can be replicated or used as a source of inspiration. In each chapter you will also find an abundance of imaginative and creative ideas that can be used in any Early Years or Key Stage 1 setting and many of the ideas can be used by childminders and at home.

The Boys' Writing Projects – underlying principles

The boys' writing projects set out to research: *'How can we improve boys' confidence, motivation and attainment as writers?'* They were designed around the following principles:

Principle 1. Effective literacy learning and teaching *is rooted in research into how young children develop and learn. It acknowledges that boys are as competent and able as girls but that they often learn in different ways and at a different pace.*

  The role of the Early Years practitioner incorporates a range of complex skills needed to facilitate children's active construction of meaning and to teach children in the way that they learn best – through play. The skilled adult has a good understanding of how young children learn typically, how boys and girls might learn differently and how individual children learn best. They have a good understanding of how children learn language and literacy skills and aptitudes. They are able to support the process of learning through child-initiated play and adult-led teaching: planning and identifying opportunities for learning, providing suitable and stimulating resources, and engaging in play, modelling reasons to write. They make learning enjoyable and motivating for children and help children to build 'learning power' (Claxton 2005).

  At the centre of the role of the Early Years practitioner is the ability to observe children in their play and to use the observations to set up enabling environments.

Principle 2. Enabling environments for young writers *offer flexible, non-prescriptive and responsive learning spaces, indoors and outdoors, that allow for the active and energetic learning styles displayed by many boys.*

  An enabling learning environment is stimulating and purposeful, and is appropriate for the learning styles and stage of development of all children. As part of an enabling environment, practitioners create sustained time for child-initiated learning. They provide accessible challenging, open-ended resources that can be used playfully, creatively and imaginatively, supporting the characteristics of effective learning that underpin writing development as well as all other areas of learning (DFE, 2012).

Introduction

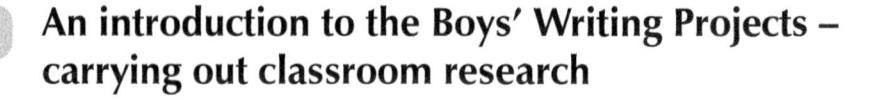

An introduction to the Boys' Writing Projects – carrying out classroom research

Practitioners went on tailored training supplemented by additional reading, and they then designed their own piece of classroom research to bring together theory and practice.

Stage 1. Auditing provision and practice

The initial stage of the classroom research involved:

- Making observations of the boys
- Making an audit of resources available to support writing
- Observing where children chose to access and use these resources independently
- Checking out how and where adults were supporting children's writing.

1.1. Starting with observation

Practitioners began the project by making observations of the boys, to find out where they chose to go, what they chose to do, the language they used in their play and their styles of play and learning. The reality for many Early Years practitioners is that they feel pressured to work from paper-led planning if they are to satisfy perceived or explicit requirements of heads and Ofsted inspectors. The result of this is that practitioners can be overly focused on using observations simply to assess children against standardized scale points, despite the emphasis that the EYFS places on observational assessment.

However, the writing projects showed that, when practitioners moved away from making simple 'tick list' observations for their assessments and started to make open observations of the boys in their self-directed play, they got to know the boys better and they learnt about the kinds of things that fascinated them – such as rocket man, blog stations, sinking sand and other things that are outside the experiences of most Early Years practitioners! The power of implementing such an approach was noted by one practitioner after one week: *'It's already paying off. There has been an increased emphasis on observing all children's interests closely. This allowed us to plan activities which the children have been really excited by and interested in.'* Another practitioner explained how the project has influenced her practice: *'We're approaching role play by thinking 'what do we want the children to get out of it?' rather than 'what shall we put in the role play area?'*

1.2. Auditing resources for writing

Opportunities to introduce a reason to write into children's play can be lost if resources aren't easily available. Practitioners made an audit of their current provision, to find out if resources for writing were inviting, readily accessible and inspiring for the boys.

1.3. The role of the adult in supporting learning

Practitioners observed the way adults interacted with the boys to motivate them to write and help them to practice their newly learned skills in their play.

1.4. Case studies

At the start of the projects, each practitioner chose two boys who, for some reason, were reluctant writers, and they observed these boys closely throughout the project. Drawing on their observations, they introduced changes to help them to become more confident writers.

Stage 2. Action planning

During the second stage of the project, practitioners chose priorities for their action plan based on their observations and audits.

When practitioners looked at their learning environments with fresh eyes, they had something of a shock. For many, there was a significant mismatch between what they were discovering about the boys' natural learning styles, and their provision, particularly in the Reception and Year 1 classes. For example, although they knew that boys (and girls) learn best when they can be active, when their learning has real purpose for them, when they can move from inside to outside and can initiate their own play, there was still a belief that children needed to sit down on the carpet or at a table to be taught writing (usually seen by teachers as letter formation and phonics) in a group. The fact that boys might be motivated by superhero play or gun play was acknowledged but this type of play was generally marginalized. In some cases, it was tolerated, but not always used effectively to enhance learning.

Practitioners began to make changes to their provision as identified in their action plans.

Stage 3. Evaluation and planning future developments

The third stage of the project was to evaluate how the changes to the learning environment (resources, space and adults) were impacting on boys' learning, especially their writing.

Learning from the Boys' Writing Projects

In Chapter 1, we investigate what is involved in learning to write, identifying developmental stages that children move through in learning to write. We explore what children need to understand and be able to do, physically, cognitively and creatively in order to write. This chapter also considers links between learning to write and children's personal, social and emotional development and considers the importance of play in supporting children's learning.

The following chapters describe the classroom research undertaken by practitioners during the projects, showing how they adapted their provision to match the learning needs and styles of individual children.

Chapter 2 draws on the characteristics of effective learning (DFE, 2012) to ask what an enabling environment for early writers should look like, and we learn how to create a 'writing playground'.

In Chapter 3, we consider how 'listening to children' can help practitioners to support children's confidence and motivation as writers, as they develop their writer's voice. We discover some of the themes, activities and resources that inspire boys to write in their play.

Chapter 4 shows how children can learn about the many purposes for writing and we find out how practitioners used children's interests to create contexts and opportunities for writing in child-initiated play and in routines.

Chapter 5 explores the complex role of the adult in motivating all children to write and teaching writing skills in a creative and playful environment. We find out about some inspiring planned activities and some thoughtful responses to children's spontaneous learning.

In Chapter 6, we see how writing skills can be developed across all curriculum areas when children are offered stimulating and open-ended learning opportunities. We discover some ideas for writing in the Prime and Specific areas of learning and development.

Finally, in Chapter 7 we see how children's first experiences of literacy at home can be used as a foundation for learning in Early Years settings and we explore ways to bridge the gap between the home learning environment and the setting.

The projects showed that boys in particular, but all children, learn better when we build our Early Years provision on a genuine understanding of how children develop and learn *typically* (from a knowledge of child development) and *as individuals* (from observations). They learn most effectively when we harness and channel their natural energy and desire to explore and make sense of the world, rather than trying to suppress these powerful learning forces in order to focus on formal academic learning at too young an age.

When I visited one Reception class in Oxfordshire, the teacher was bubbling with enthusiasm: *'So much has happened, I don't know where to start!'* I felt the same when I started to write this book. There are so many positive, heart-warming, individual and collective stories to share and it is a particular privilege to share these at a time when the focus in so much of the education world is on 'targets' and 'outcomes'. Many of the findings were obvious in hindsight, simple to implement, highly enjoyable for children and practitioners – *and* they resulted in significantly improved attainment for boys in writing.

1 Write from the start

> Daisy, aged 2, clambers up onto a chair at the kitchen table and picks up a pencil. She gives a deep sigh, lowers her head and starts to make marks on some paper. Her mother looks up, surprised, then realizes that Daisy is copying the tense posture that she often has when she writes.
>
> George, aged 4, holds his drawing above his head and says: 'Who wants this? Someone who's been very good today!'

Learning to write is vital if we are to take part successfully in the adult world. When we are at ease with the written word, we can gather and retain ideas and information, we can create and enjoy stories and communicate simple and complex messages with others. But the importance of writing isn't obvious to very young children. They learn how to 'join the literacy club' (Smith, 1988) from positive, caring role models who are already part of the club: family members, friends and people in the community who write for all kinds of purposes as part of their working and home life.

By the time children start school, they will have absorbed attitudes to writing from their early experiences, and they will reflect back at the world the positive and negative experiences that have been presented to them. Early literacy provision can only be effective if it allows children to gain a positive view of themselves as writers while they acquire the necessary skills to communicate through writing.

What does early writing look like?

When Amie started in her Reception class, she could recite the alphabet confidently and she loved spending time at the writing table, filling sheets of paper with neatly formed letter shapes copied from the alphabet chart. Her mother was very proud of the 'work' that she brought home at the end of the day. When her teacher sat with Amie and gently encouraged her to talk about her writing, Amie was unresponsive. For Amie, the enjoyment was in creating the shapes and patterns on the page, and having her mother's approval. She hadn't yet understood that writing was a way of communicating a message and she hadn't made the connection between the alphabet that she could chant with the letters that she could write on the page.

Jack spends most of his time in the Reception class outside, playing games connected with space travel. He is fascinated by meteorites and often brings books about space travel to school. He creates complex play narratives with his friends involving conflicts that he resolves with aliens and other space travellers.

Who is the better writer, Amie who produces pages filled with well-formed letter shapes, or Jack, who doesn't choose to write on paper, but is articulate and imaginative?

Early experiences

In order to become a writer, children must develop *transcriptional skills* of handwriting, spelling and punctuation; and they must develop *compositional skills*, by finding a creative and expressive voice of their own which they can communicate using the transcriptional skills of writing.

The foundations of writing are in spoken language. Children who have rich experiences of oral language absorb the rhythms and patterns of everyday speech and learn the language of stories, rhymes and songs. They learn to express their thoughts, ideas and feelings orally and to enter into other worlds.

Children can start to develop a voice of their own as a writer from very young, in the company of caring adults who listen to their voice and encourage them to express themselves.

Role play

When children play with small world characters and engage in role play they are beginning to create stories. Sophia, aged 2 years and 10 months, is using language to develop her thinking and to make sense of her world as she plays with cars at the kitchen table.

> 'Vroom, vroom, vroom, vroom . . .' (She shunts the cars)
>
> 'Hallo!' 'Look at my handstand.' (The two cars are talking to each other)
>
> 'Look dad. Come play with me. Dad! Daddy car, look! Daddy car, come play with me.'
>
> 'Having a bath!' (She puts the car in a cup of milk)
>
> 'One car called Dylan, one called mummy, one called daddy.'
>
> 'Slurp, slurp, slurp!' (She feeds the car, singing)

Sophia's use of private speech (Vygotsky, 1962) allows us to see that she has created characters for the cars based on her family (Dylan is her little brother) and she is acting out the familiar events of meal times, bath times and play with Daddy. Within a few years, Sophia's private speech will become internalized as thought or 'inner speech' (Vygotsky, 1962), and as she grows older, she will be able to create stories and compose her thoughts internally. In university libraries, adults can read and write in silence. In Early Years classrooms, a quiet space is unproductive. Young children need to use language to think and learn.

Playing with songs, rhymes and stories

Adults can help children to develop a writer's voice by reading the same stories and singing the same songs repeatedly. Playing with stories, songs and rhymes, using familiar structures to create new versions by changing some of the words is a simple way to show children that they can be authors, poets and songwriters.

Scribing

When adults scribe children's words as they draw or play, or while they make cards for friends and family, children begin to see the connection between their oral language and the conventions of written language. They are now becoming members of the 'literacy club'.

The transcriptional skills involved in writing will inevitably come later than compositional skills. Children start to make the connection between sounds they hear and the symbolic representation of these sounds when they see writing modelled by adults in contexts that make sense to them and when they become aware of writing around them at home, in shops and in the street.

Children can engage in the 'whole act' of writing before they understand the mechanics of spelling and punctuation, when they give meaning to marks that they make in their play. But at some stage, the mechanics do need to be taught directly, when children are at the appropriate stage of development to make sense of a symbolic system.

Developmental stages in learning the transcriptional skills of writing

1. Ascribes meaning to marks

Children start to make marks and give meaning to them when they mimic adults who they see writing, just as they mimic adults who cook or drive a car. They are likely to do this if inviting writing materials are freely available and if adults comment on their own writing and respond to children's attempts sensitively and with encouragement.

When children start to give meaning to their marks they are beginning to understand that writing is a way of recording speech in a symbolic form. Vincenzo's writing is at this stage. He has a purpose for his writing – he is writing an order for some shoes in the role play shoe shop. His writing flows

Write from the start

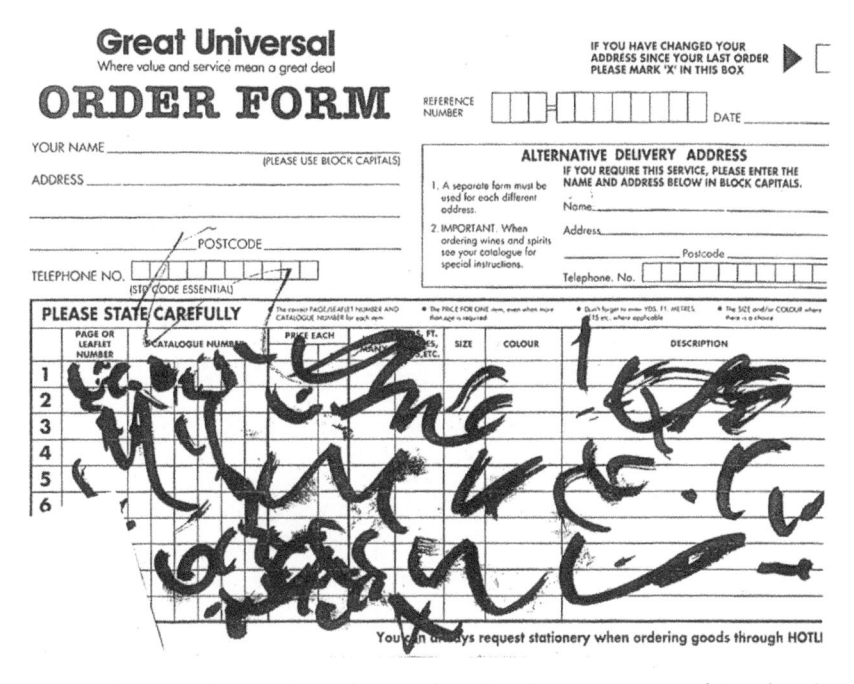

Figure 1.1 Example 1: Independent mark making by Vincenzo, aged 3, in his play

fluently, but he hasn't used any conventional letter shapes, as he doesn't yet understand the symbolic system used in writing English.

2. Uses some letter-like shapes and identifiable letters to communicate meaning

Conventional letter shapes and letter-like shapes start to appear in children's writing when children and adults start to write together and when adults comment on writing around them: in the child's name, in shops, on buses, in newspapers. Children should be encouraged to make marks and the adult can scribe the child's words, modelling how to form letter shapes.

Aalia uses a mixture of letter shapes and numbers, which she has seen in books and in the environment around her. An adult has shown her the letters in her name and these appear frequently in her writing. She hasn't yet made the link between sounds (phonemes) and the letters (graphemes) that are used to represent the sounds.

Write from the start

Figure 1.2 Example 2: Independent writing by a 3-year-old girl, Aalia, following a group session when the adult modelled writing a letter to Barty Bear

3. Uses some clearly identifiable letters to communicate meaning, representing some sounds correctly

Cayley has composed a letter and written a name on the envelope. She has begun to link the sounds that she hears with some of the written symbols that represent the sounds when she writes the first letter in each word. She has taken an enormous step forward in her understanding of the transcriptional

Figure 1.3 Example 3: Independent writing by Cayley, aged 4 years. She has written a letter: *D M* (Dear Mum), *W Y E K T G* (Would you like (to) come to Grandpont) – which she has put in an envelope and written *J M* (Julie's Mum)

6

Write from the start

aspect of writing, and now recognizes that writing is a symbolic code that she will be able to learn and use to communicate with others.

Like Vincenzo and Aalia, Cayley has joined the 'literacy club'. It is at this stage that phonics teaching becomes really relevant. Cayley is now ready to build up her bank of letters and sounds, to learn the conventions of spelling, and to learn some commonly used phonetically irregular words so that she can develop her independent writing.

4. Uses phonic knowledge to write words in ways which match their spoken sounds

Arlo started to write and illustrate his story spontaneously and unaided during the free-flow session in his nursery school. He chose to sit at a table and write about a subject that interested him; he chose the paper to write on, and the pencil to write with; and he chose when to start writing and when to stop

Figure 1.4 Example 4: Independent writing by Arlo, aged 4 *Wus pon tum* (Once upon a time) *Livt L Fri bes* (lived the three bears) *bEbE bAEy mumE* (baby bear mummy)

7

Write from the start

writing. He drew on his knowledge of traditional stories and story conventions and he used story language, as distinct from conversational language. He stopped when the physical act of writing became tiring, which happened to be before the end of the story.

5. Writes simple sentences which can be read by themselves and others. Some words are spelt correctly and others are phonetically plausible

Simon is able to express himself through writing that can be read by others, and which includes some learnt spellings. He will continue to refine his writing skills as his reading ability and spoken language develop, and his written language will become correspondingly more complex.

Figure 1.5 Example 5: Diary written by Simon, aged 5

Developmentally appropriate early writing

In the Early Years, we must be wary of placing too much emphasis on transcriptional aspects of writing too early as this can cause confusion and can create negative attitudes towards writing. Cody's experience shows how this can happen.

> Cody is taking part in a phonics session in a Reception class. The children are given cards with letter shapes written on them and the teacher asks them which sound their letter makes. Cody holds his card, which has a large S on it, to his ear. *'Nope, I can't hear anything,'* he says.

Cody has not yet made the link between phonemes and graphemes. At this developmental stage, he needs plenty of encouragement to make marks and to give his marks meaning in his play – perhaps writing a sign for the superhero shop.

Lillian Katz (2011: 125–6) refers to the 'damaged disposition hypothesis' when children learn formal skills too early, damaging the disposition to use the skills. She reports on research by Rebecca Marcon which shows that children, especially boys, do less well in academic Early Years programmes, compared with High/Scope – perhaps because 'boys do not so easily accept being placed in the passive role that is implied in the academic curriculum approach.' (quoted in Katz, 2011: 126)

The boys' writing projects showed that, when we focus on developing compositional aspects of writing in play, children become motivated to write. Children who are positively disposed to write can be guided through the developmental stages of writing towards conventional spelling and punctuation. Practitioners taking part in the boys' writing projects consistently described their boys as reluctant writers when asked to write by an adult, particularly if the writing was at a table. When writing opportunities were moved to the places where boys chose to play and were included in the boys' play, they became keen and motivated writers.

When children have the motivation and confidence to write, then the job of teaching them transcriptional skills becomes straightforward. If we try and teach skills to children who haven't understood their purpose, then it becomes a struggle for the child and the practitioner, and is likely to make children less effective learners.

Finding a voice: Developing compositional writing skills

> Rachel is a screenplay writer, and she describes how she tackles the job of writing.
>
> *'When I start to imagine a plot and build up characters, I think about the times when I played with Sylvanian animals when I was small. Each Sylvanian had a particular character and the narrative evolved as I moved them around. Screenplay writing is very similar.'*

Whichever developmental stage children are at in terms of transcriptional aspects of writing, they can develop their compositional skills as writers if we listen to them and join them as they play. If we expect children to spend too much time mastering and using the transcriptional aspects of writing, this is likely to hinder the development of their writer's voice, as writing becomes a

Figure 1.6 A child is writing with his teacher outside

task done for the teacher, with no intrinsic value. The following scenario shows how one teacher reflected on her practice to inspire her class to become motivated and imaginative writers.

A Reception/Year 1/Year 2 class in a small village school

During a literacy lesson in March, the children discussed the things they knew about Spring and they made a list of words together. Then the children were asked to write a poem in pairs, starting each line with the words: *Spring is* . . . The teacher scribed for some younger children, and others wrote independently at their own level. Watching the children write, it was evident that each child was picking a word from the list and writing a sentence in turn, without any collaboration, discussion or creative thinking.

The teacher recognized that the activity had little meaning for the children, who were keen to finish their task and then do something that did interest them. She asked herself: how can the children be encouraged to draw on their own ideas and imagination in their creative writing?

A few weeks later, the class was taking part in a literacy lesson while they were learning about castles.

The children were all outside. They had built a large castle together from plastic construction pieces, and they had made props for role play, such as swords, shields and trebuchets. When they were ready, they wrote stories based on their role play, lying comfortably on the grass, writing on clipboards, with an adult scribing for them or writing independently. One child wrote (scribed by an adult):

'I fought a bad knight. The battle happened near the castle. I used a sword. I still don't know who is going to win the battle.'

She didn't know who was going to win the battle because she hadn't played the scenario out yet. When she finished her role play she completed her story.

Other pieces of creative writing based on the Castle theme included writing a list of things that the servants and the princesses did:

continued

Write from the start

Survents
Surve king and queens breakfast.
Killing the animals for dinner.
Setting the fires

1 beeing a Surfent!
2 Surve king and queens breakfast dinner and supper
3 Give king and queen bath
4 Making beds for king and queen
5 Killing the animals for dinner and supper and breakfast
6 Setting the fires
7 Sending the messegs
8 Washing up king and queens clothes
9 Making king and queens clothes
10 fetch the skin the wool and the food
11 fetch the wepens
12 clean the castle
Brett Massey
Bronte R
Amelia R

Figure 1.7 Servants

> **Princesses**
> *The princess dusoot get drest by herself.*
> *Princesses are stropy if they stey up leat.*
> *The princess is lesyaz.*
> Another child had written a warning sign:
> *I men it im going to et you up!*
>
> The princess mite have hur brecfust in bed.
>
> The princess mite tell the suvunts off.
>
> The princess is lesyaz.
>
> The princess dusoot get drest by hurself.
>
> Princesses are stropy if they stey up leat.
>
> By Honor and Molly Juno
>
> *Figure 1.8* Princesses

Every piece of writing was individual and reflected the children's own voices and imagination. The children were fully engaged and came up with their own thoughts, suggestions and comments, which were all valued by the teacher. So what had the teacher done to bring about such a significant change?

First, the writing was now part of the children's play, rather than a task to be completed before they could play, and it had intrinsic interest for the children. Second, the emphasis was on the creative aspect of writing and the children were given help and support to write so that they were able to record their stories and ideas. The teacher had matched her provision to the children's interests and was working with their natural way of learning rather than expecting children to adapt to the expectations of school learning.

Play is children's natural mechanism for learning as it allows them to construct their own understandings about the world around them: there is no dichotomy between play-based learning and academic learning.

> *The power of play as the engine of learning in early childhood and as a vital force for young children's physical, social, and emotional development is beyond question. Children in play-based kindergartens have a double advantage over those who are denied play: they end up equally good or better at reading and other intellectual skills, and they are more likely to become well-adjusted healthy people.*
>
> Miller and Almon (2009: 8)

Children can learn formal, academic skills through play when a skilled adult is there to support and scaffold children's learning, as evidence from the boys' writing projects shows. Play supports both short-term and long-term mastery by allowing children to learn *about writing* in contexts that make sense to them in the short term, and to learn *to write* by applying and practising taught skills, embedding the learning. The academic skills that children learn through play become the foundation for learning future skills, and foster learning dispositions that enhance children's learning through to their adult life.

The projects helped practitioners to reflect on their role in supporting opportunities for writing in play as well as in adult-led teaching. Practitioners went alongside the children in their play and sensitively introduced contextualized writing opportunities, such as a list of jobs for the mechanic, or making a sign for the Ice Cream Shop. Children who were reluctant to write in a formal context were often keen to write in situations that they found non-threatening.

The following scenario shows how a child was finding his voice as a writer at home.

> Zak, aged 3, and Tom, aged 18 months are brothers. Their mother described how she went into their shared bedroom and found that Zak had written one word on each of the three drawers in his cupboard:

> *Zak and Tom*
>
> Zak's mother was delighted that he was able to write his name and his brother's name and was especially proud that he had written *and* – but she was also worried that he had written on the furniture. Zak's mother wanted to allow him to have a writer's voice while helping him to learn conventions about writing: that it is acceptable to write on some things and not on others. She solved the problem by giving him some Post-it notes and small pieces of card and Blu-tack. She then allowed him to write labels on the Post-its and card and put them around the house.

Every child can be a writer

During a workshop for Nursery parents on early writing, one mother proudly told the other parents about her daughter, who loved making tiny books for her dolls, filling them with her mark making and drawings. When she heard this, another mother burst into tears. 'Connor doesn't ever want to write,' she sobbed. 'He's going to have such problems when he starts school.'

We have started to put enormous pressure on young children (and their parents) by expecting them to become competent transcriptional writers in order to meet the 'school readiness agenda'. Children in the Early Years are still developing the gross and fine motor skills required to sit still, hold a pencil and form letter shapes on paper. Writing can be a painful process when letter formation is emphasized over the message being communicated. As we have seen, this is especially problematic when children haven't yet understood that the letter shapes that they are being asked to write are a symbolic representation of spoken language. For many children, and in particular many boys such as Aiden, writing becomes disturbing and painful.

They keep asking me to look down at my paper and I just want to look up sometimes.

The boys' writing projects showed that children will become more confident writers as well as doing better in standardized assessments if we stop educating 'from the neck up' (Ken Robinson, at the TEDx conference, London, 2011) and trust their innate drive to explore and make sense of their world. Project practitioners created learning environments (a combination of space, resources, adult support and time) that were in tune with children's stage of development and natural ways of learning. The key elements that allowed every child to become a writer are all central to excellent Early Years practice:

- Practitioners used their observations of the children and audits of the writing provision to create opportunities where children could experience writing for different purposes in all areas of the classroom provision, inside and outside, in contexts that had meaning for them
- Children were given plenty of time to write in their play supported by adults who understood how children learn to write and were able to help children to see how writing could enhance their play
- Adults became positive role models for the children, modelling creative writing and writing for many different practical purposes.

Conclusion

If we would listen to our kids, we'd discover that they are largely self-explanatory.

Robert Brault (n.d.)

Ken Spours (TEDx conference, London, 2011) argued that education is too important to be treated as a political football, with politicians determining what happens in schools. The boys' writing projects placed the educational 'football' back in the hands (or at the feet) of the practitioners, as they became involved in their own observation-led classroom research. In the following chapters, we see that it became normal in the boys' writing project settings to find children – boys and girls – spontaneously writing *everywhere*. The more they wrote creatively, the more they understood the value and purpose of writing, so they became motivated and willing to invest the time needed to improve their transcriptional skills. The project practitioners were able to show colleagues, head teachers and Year 1 teachers that an educational approach based in child development, a good understanding of the developmental stages in learning to write and observational assessment works!

In Chapter 2, we discover how project practitioners changed and developed their learning environments to give children inspiring resources and opportunities to write.

> *I felt demoralized at the beginning of the project, now I feel recharged, able to work in the way I know is best.*

2 Creating a writing-rich environment

We value writing anytime, any place, anywhere.

In Chapter 1 we considered how very young children start to become writers alongside involved, caring adults and through the most effective and developmentally appropriate learning mechanism, play. In this chapter we explore how the physical environment can be developed as the 'third educator' (Rinaldi, 2006). We see how the provision of inspiring resources can motivate children to write. We discover that deep levels of learning are achieved when children are self-motivated and when they have the space and time to practise taught writing skills; and we learn about some practical ways to create a writing playground, where children find writing irresistible.

An enabling environment

The following observations of two boys, both equally able, took place in the same Reception classroom.

> Ollie was making a model independently:
>
> *'I don't know what to play with, it's all fun!'*
>
> He started to build a Lego model, talking to an adult about what he was making.

Creating a writing-rich environment

> *'It's a space rocket what can drive and when there's a train what's in danger and the train jumps on the track and the person can go in it. Then the train goes down back to Earth, cos someone's shot the train up to Space. And the train didn't like it. And the person saved it up in Space.*
>
> *There's some fire under the wheels and the fire gets hotter and hotter and when the person counts up to 6 it blasts off and it stays up for 30 minutes and then goes down straight away.*
>
> *It's tricky to make it. I'm trying really hard to mend it.'*

Contrast Ollie's play and learning with the following observation.

> George was completing a writing task with an adult.
>
> George: *'I'm writing "mouse is walking".'* He wrote an 'm' on his page.
> Teacher: *'Can you hear any other sounds?'*
> George: *'ou.'* He found the 'ou' sound on his sound card and copied it.
>
> *'I'm tired. I didn't get much sleep.'*

In the first observation, Ollie's lively commentary reflects his involvement in his narrative as the words tumble out. He expressed his own thoughts and ideas and enjoyed the complexity of the task and the element of struggle and problem solving. He was confident and relaxed.

In the second observation, George sat at a table with a hunched posture, losing concentration easily, showing little interest in his task.

Observations such as these can help practitioners to see if their provision is helping or hindering children's learning. What were the conditions that allowed one boy to exude excitement as he created his complex narrative, while, in the same classroom, another boy struggled to focus and express himself?

Mihaly Csikszentmihalyi (2002) would have described Ollie's absorption in his task as reflecting a state of 'flow', a state that is characterized by total immersion in an activity because of the *intrinsic* rewards it offers. Ferre Laevers' Wellbeing and Involvement scales (2005) enable practitioners to observe and measure the extent to which young children are working in a state of 'flow', where Wellbeing is defined as 'Like a fish in water' (Laevers, 2005:

6) and Involvement is defined as being 'completely absorbed' by an activity. When there are high levels of Wellbeing and Involvement 'we know children are operating at the very limits of their capabilities. Because of all these qualities involvement is the condition that brings about deep level learning' (Laevers, 2005: 10).

Analysis of observations of children using Wellbeing and Involvement scales can indicate how well the environment is meeting children's learning needs.

> *The use of this self-evaluation instrument not only leads to significant changes in the settings . . . It also contributes to the professional development of practitioners. Through the process they learn to take the perspective of the child in their approach and because of this to create optimal conditions for the social-emotional and cognitive development of children.*
>
> Laevers (2005: 4)

Matching provision to the learning needs of children

Reflecting on the learning environment

In the Statutory Framework for the Early Years Foundation Stage, *characteristics of effective learning* are defined as: *'Playing and exploring; Active learning; and Creating and thinking critically'* (DFE, 2012: 7). During the boys' writing projects, practitioners focused on *how* children learn, as well as *what* children learn in order to create stimulating, challenging and inclusive environments that promote effective learning for all children.

The classroom has been described as the 'third educator' (Rinaldi, 2006), where the *space, quality and accessibility of resources* and *time to pursue learning* all contribute to the effectiveness of learning. At the start of the boys' writing projects, practitioners made an audit of resources that were available in all areas of the continuous provision to encourage oral language development and mark making (see Appendix 2). At the same time they tracked and observed the boys, to find out how they chose to use the space and resources in the learning environment independently. The aim was to discover how effective the environment was in stimulating and motivating boys to develop their oral and written language in imaginative and creative play.

Practitioners found that there was a tendency for most writing to take place during formal, adult-led activities. Writing tasks were set by an adult; they were done at specific times (decided by the practitioner); and they took place in specific places (usually at tables, inside). Role play, creative play and spontaneous mark making in play were less well-supported by adults. This meant that opportunities to extend children's language, thinking and writing skills were sometimes missed, and children's preoccupations went unobserved.

So when practitioners used their observations and audits to look at their learning environments with fresh eyes, many of them found a mismatch between what they were discovering about boys' natural learning styles, and their provision, especially in the Reception classes. Although they knew that boys (and girls) learn best when they can be active, when their learning has real purpose for them, when they can move from inside to outside and when they can initiate their own play, there was still a belief that the best way to teach writing (usually seen by teachers as letter formation and phonics) was to a group of children, on the carpet or at a table. However, observations showed that children were rarely applying their taught skills in their play.

What did practitioners discover about how boys used the learning environment from their observations?

Observations showed that, in general:

- Boys didn't choose to write at tables – they would come and do some writing with an adult when they were asked to, but these tasks were usually seen as something they *had* to do before they were allowed to play
- They rarely went to the book corner and when they did, it often was to engage in rough and tumble play
- They spent a lot of time outside
- Their play was very physical, active and they used a lot of space, moving constantly
- They enjoyed playing with construction materials and on the computer.

These were common findings in every setting – pre-schools, nurseries and Reception classes. Of course there were exceptions, and some boys loved sitting in the book corner looking at books, or chose to write at a table. But these boys were already fitting into the school system and were making

Creating a writing-rich environment

progress with their writing and reading. The projects aimed to find ways to support the boys who *didn't* fit into the current system.

What did practitioners discover about the quality of the learning environment from their audits?

When practitioners audited their learning environment to find out how well resourced they were for mark making and writing materials, they discovered many positives, but there were also some general issues that emerged:

Space: almost every setting had a writing area and book corner, but in many settings, these areas were small and under-resourced. There was little incentive for children to use these areas as part of their play.

Resources: role play, writing and mark making resources were limited and weren't linked to children's recurrent play themes. Mark making and writing resources needed sorting and labelling to allow children to be more independent.

Displays: more environmental print was needed. Many settings had no display boards where children could show their independent writing.

Time: in some settings, the sessions were very structured, with only short periods of time for sustained child-initiated play and learning.

Intervention studies described by Fisher et al. (2011) show that young children's learning becomes more profound and long-lasting when literacy resources are put into the play environment. In these studies, the children in the intervention group were more likely to initiate literacy activities in their play, and they spent longer in more complex literacy-related activities than children in the control group. When project practitioners developed their provision to reflect children's learning needs and interests and when resources could be accessed independently to support autonomous play there was an immediate impact on the children's willingness to write, spontaneously or with a little encouragement, in their play. Of course, the resources alone were not enough. It was also important to make sure that all adults were listening and interacting with the children and tuning into opportunities for writing that occurred in children's self-initiated play. This challenge is looked at in detail in Chapter 5.

> The following observation of two three year olds was made in a small village pre-school where a new writing trolley had been placed outside.
> Lennon was making a model with small wooden blocks: 'We're making something.'
> Kyle picked up a small pad and pencil from the writing trolley and made some marks on the first page: 'And I'm checking we've got everything we need. I'm just checking we got all the things we need to make a big tower. We need pixes and mixes and willins and billins. You got all the stuff you need, Lennon, you can stop working now.'

We've met our aim of achieving a 'writing culture'. All the staff can see it. The thing that's done it is having writing everywhere.

Active learning

It was evident that many boys needed to be physically active and on the move. Sally Goddard Blyth reminds us that the 'most advanced level of movement is the ability to stay totally still' (N. Rowe, quoted in Goddard Blythe, 2005: 137) so children who find it hard to sit still need to move *more*, not less, in order to develop mature motor skills. The writing projects found that, when resources for writing were extended into active play provision, boys became keen to mark make and write and their writing began to add a new dimension to their imaginative play.

Rena Upitis uses the term 'music playground' to describe music-rich Early Years provision. Many of the characteristics of a music playground are common to literacy-rich environments, including 'an emphasis on the processes of learning; a nurturing atmosphere in which it is safe to take risks; choice and collaboration are encouraged' and where the environment is 'physically inviting' (quoted in Pound and Harrison 2003: 97). By analogy, we can describe the learning environments created during the boys' writing projects as 'writing playgrounds'.

Creating opportunities for writing everywhere

The children were enthused by the changes to the environment!

Supporting speaking and listening

> Children in a literate society learn of 'reading as one way of listening and of writing as one way of talking.'
>
> Taylor (1983: 87)

In pre-literate societies, stories, information and knowledge are shared and passed on orally. In literate societies, young children need to develop oral skills of describing and recounting, creating and telling a story, giving explanations and instructions, and arguing a point of view and these oral skills can then be translated into literacy skills – writing and interpreting text. The writing projects focused on speaking and listening skills, especially with the 3- and 4-year-old children, as well as mark making and writing skills. Bilingual and bi-literate support allowed children learning English as an additional language to develop their first language skills in their play, and to improve their English in context.

Resources that work well to support oral language development include:

- Small-world play
- Puppets
- Storyboards, story sacks and story props – children can retell familiar stories in their own words, in their own time, and in their first language if they are EAL learners
- Open-ended resources which can be used flexibly and creatively by different children – such as, large cardboard boxes, cardboard tubes, different types of material in a range of colours and sizes, hollow blocks, crates, planks
- Dressing up clothes which aren't prescriptive or gender-specific to promote imaginative play – such as cloaks in different colours
- Video cameras – children can video their performances and edit them and add captions, using stop motion software for making animated films. Children can make posters and tickets for their performances
- Digital cameras to record children's activities and document the process of learning. The photos can be made into slide shows on the computer,

printed out to make books or made into displays of activities with the children's commentary scribed alongside the photos. Children can then talk about their learning with caring adults
- 'Ask me about' display – photos of children engaged in different activities with captions, such as 'Ask me about Forest School' or 'Ask me about when we planted some seeds'.

> *What's made a difference is having open-ended resources and things that interest the boys more.*

Writing in role play

Role play areas help children to move into the 'literacy club' by creating spaces where they can use language in play contexts that link to the real world and where they can engage in symbolic play as a precursor to writing. As they begin to understand that writing is a way of recording language in a symbolic form, they can mark make and write in contexts that have intrinsic meaning for them. At the same time, role play supports social development and collaborative play.

During the project, role play themes were developed by practitioners based on observations of children's interests and preoccupations as well as in discussion with children. The areas offered a multitude of reasons for writing and reading including open/closed signs; shop signs; appointment sheets; MOT certificates; registers; price labels; prescription pads; gift tags.

Creating a writing area

Children pick up implicit messages about the value that adults place on writing and the type of writing that is valued, from the way a writing area is set up and resourced. View the writing area from the perspective of young children who have the desire and need to play – a small table with blunt pencils and a few sheets of recycled paper will struggle to compete with other more playful resources.

A well-resourced writing area will include:

- Writing materials that help children to practise both transcriptional and compositional skills of writing: paper in different sizes and colours, pencils,

Creating a writing-rich environment

  felt pens, crayons, alphabet mats, name cards, blank books, hole punches, diaries, envelopes, parcel tags
- Writing resources that are in good condition and regularly replenished
- A display board for independent writing and a message board or message boxes, where children can write messages to each other. Boards can be linked to a changing theme such as friendship: *Jasper is mi frend becos he shers his crsps* or for any messages that the children want to write. The messages can be scribed or written independently
- A post box (remember to empty it regularly!)

Introduce new, varied and unusual resources a few at a time. Have 'special' mark making tools, such as gold pens and sparkly pencils; special things to write on, such as laminated speech bubbles, 'have a go' books for independent writing and interesting shaped books.

The writing area should be a permanent part of the provision and, ideally, it will be large enough for children to move around the tables, and work collaboratively. Writing resources can also be put in dens and other special places, inside and outside. Clear a space for children to write on the floor and have a swivel chair for the child who wants to sit at a table but can't keep still!

> Two 3-year-old boys in a small pre-school were showing no interest in mark making. They were fascinated by dragons, so the pre-school staff drew some 'dragon footprints' leading into a den, where they had put some attractive mark making resources. The boys followed the footprints enthusiastically, and soon began to copy other children who were using the new mark making resources in their play.

Display

Saturate your room with writing! Create a space in the writing area or nearby where children can display their independent writing and mark making as well as displaying adult handwriting and printed text. Provide examples of writing in different languages and scripts on display boards and in all areas of the continuous provision.

Creating a writing-rich environment

Figure 2.1 Develop a 'catch me writing' culture and display photos of the children mark making or writing with scribed captions

Phonics displays and writing celebration walls have brought displays to life and raised the value of writing in children's eyes.

> A boy and a girl are facing each other through the space inside the easel, drawing on notepads for 20 minutes. The boy sings: *'I like to draw, I like to draw, I like to draw.'*

Writing on a large scale

A writing area will appeal to some children while other children prefer to mark make and write on a large scale, as this requires less refined gross and fine motor skills. During the projects, children enjoyed writing and making marks in a way that was comfortable for them. They stood up or lay on the floor. They curled up or stretched out, absorbed and motionless or kicking their heels while they worked.

Creating a writing-rich environment

Resources for large-scale writing and mark making can include:

- Large blackboards and whiteboards, inside and outside
- Interactive Whiteboards
- Pavement chalks on the ground and walls
- Paints, chalks, felt pens, fabric paints, crayons, spray bottles or washing up liquid bottles filled with coloured water or paint
- Large rolls or sheets of paper or material on the ground, walls or on tables.

A group of boys and girls were taken into a room where a long roll of plain paper had been laid out on the floor. They were invited to make marks on the paper while a piece of classical music was playing.

Immediately, the boys were very interested. When the music became faster or louder, they moved around the paper and made large marks, and when music was quieter and slower, they lay down and made smaller pictures. They tended to work alone, while the girls stayed in a small group and worked on one area of the paper.

There were high levels of involvement and the children were all keen to show their parents at the end of the session.

Leo wrote OMIJAL very carefully on a large whiteboard. *'Look what I writed.'*

Kelsey: *'Leo, Leo, what did you write?'*
Leo proclaimed: *'Who knows what I writed?'* Then he whispered to Kelsey: *'Bottom!'*

Creating a writing-rich environment

Writing outside

At the start of the projects, writing activities were usually set up inside, while the boys were choosing to play outside. Boys began to write outside when writing resources were placed strategically in the garden and when adults were on hand to suggest reasons for writing in their play.

Children have made maps inside at the mark making area and taken them outside to use in their play.

Resources that stimulate language and writing outside include:

- A well-stocked writing trolley that can be wheeled outside on a daily basis – you will find that you can stimulate and maintain excitement and interest by adding a few resources at a time
- Investigation boxes with binoculars, blank charts and checklists on laminated card and non-fiction books about minibeasts, birds or wild flowers
- Dens and hideaway places or an outdoor play house with different mark making materials inside will entice children to have a go at writing
- Laminated sheets and clipboards that can be used outside whatever the weather
- Outside book boxes with fiction and non-fiction books
- Signs and labels such as road signs to use in role play and labels for resources
- A music and movement performance area and movement play space
- Parachute games with an adult
- Forest school-type activities, such as mark making with burnt wood or sticks, or following clues as part of a treasure hunt for natural materials
- Non-permanent resources, such as water with large brushes or sprays with coloured liquid.

Noah was drawing a dragon with yellow chalk on the ground outside. He started to draw dragon footprints going into the classroom.

'He's going into the classroom!'

Other children picked up on his contagious excitement and followed him.

Noah: *He's been down here!'* (He pointed to the path that went alongside the classroom) *'He's drawn some breadcrumbs!'* (He drew some spots.)
Liam: *'Another one! ANOTHER one!'*
Noah: *'He's left breadcrumbs!'* (He drew lots of spots) *'The footprints changed colour, the footprints changed colour, the footprints changed colour! It's gone blue!'* (He started drawing with blue chalk.)
Ollie: *'There's another one there! It's a baby one!'*
Noah: (drawing tiny footprints) *'It's an even babier one!'*
Ollie: (drawing a big footprint) *'There's a daddy one!'*
Liam: *'It's a massive one!'*

Figure 2.2 Noah is drawing a dragon as part of his play

Creating a writing-rich environment

> Noah: (excitedly) 'He's been walking all over the place! There's an even massiver one here!'
> Ollie: (He drew some footprints on the gate that led to the pre-school.) 'He creeped . . .! He climbed the wall thing! Aaaaah! Aaaaah! He's chasing us! He's right under there! He changed colour, he went pink!'
> Liam: (drew footprints on a car) 'O–oh, he's in the car.' (This was followed by lots of squeals from the crowd of children.)
> Ollie: 'He was climbing everywhere!'
> Noah: 'Get out the car, he might dragonfly you!'
>
> Later, inside the classroom, Noah saw a chalk mark on a table and asked: 'How did he wander inside?'

'Writing on the move' resources

Children liked to move between the inside and outside areas and, when mobile writing materials were made available, children were able to write everywhere. They took writing materials into dens, under tables, into the sandpit, under the climbing frame. Effective 'writing on the move' resources include:

- Small laminated writing pads on key rings, to attach to children's clothes
- Small clipboards and whiteboards
- Writing bats
- Writing rucksacks, belts, tool boxes, lunch boxes, buckets or other interesting mobile containers, filled with mark making tools, paper and pads, walkie-talkies or mobile phones.

Hari has a clipboard surgically attached to him! He's so fascinated by writing that it encourages others to join in. He's so proud of himself.

Writing belts, clipboards and writing toolboxes have had the most impact on writing for boys and girls.

Boys like clipboards to record what they can see through binoculars.

Creating a writing-rich environment

Book sharing

Initial observations showed that boys often used book corners for active play and for building models, so practitioners thought creatively about how they could make book sharing an integral part of children's everyday experience. Fiction and non-fiction books were placed in all areas of the continuous provision and specific books were chosen and displayed, linked to the children's observed interests. Beanbags and mats were placed in book corners to make a cosy area for quiet reading and imaginative reading dens were created inside and outside.

Book areas can be filled with:

- Home-made books made by children alone or in groups: tiny books and giant books; flap books; how to . . . books such as *How to grow sunflowers*; tactile books; books about routines
- Books with props – story sacks, puppets, small world
- Dual-language books
- Story and song CDs.

> After reading *Whatever Next* by Jill Murphy to the children, the nursery teacher left the book in the book corner next to a cardboard box, a colander and a pair of wellington boots. Jason took control and decided he was going to go to the moon, with the 'space helmet' colander on his head, and the 'space boots' on his feet. Another child brought a playdough picnic and they went 'up the chimney' to the moon together.

Writing in all areas of provision

Mark making and writing resources are available everywhere, all the time.

Practitioners saturated their learning environments with writing resources and print so that reading and writing became a normal, everyday experience.

Creating a writing-rich environment

Literacy resources for all areas of the continuous provision can include:

- The home corner – recipe cards, newspapers with crossword grids, newspapers in different languages, catalogues with blank forms, shopping lists, calendars
- The construction area – architects' plans, clip boards and large sheets of paper on the wall where children can draw designs, construction certificates, labels for models
- The workshop area – boxes with different scripts and in different languages to use for model making, sticky labels for children to write about their models
- By the computer – a list where children can write their name when they are waiting for a turn
- In a play house outside – a book box, laminated sheets, clipboards and pens.

Fine motor development

Writing on whiteboards is popular because of the temporary nature of the writing.

Children enjoyed developing the fine motor skills necessary for writing using a range of different resources. To support fine motor development, provide:

- Sensory materials, such as gloop, cornflour, mud, wet and dry sand, salt, rice, shaving foam and on velvet material, with fingers and mark making tools
- Finger painting with paint – or drinking chocolate!
- Paint or fabric crayons on large sheets of material on tables, on the floor or on the wall
- Gel boards
- Sticks in mud, coloured water in snow, cotton buds with paint or food colouring
- Water and different sized brushes outside on the ground, on walls, in builders' trays
- Sprays and washing up liquid bottles – to make trails and patterns with coloured water or paint
- Tweezers and pipettes.

Creating a writing-rich environment

> In one pre-school, a new large whiteboard proved to be a great success, as the boys spent long periods of time making marks, rubbing them out and re-doing them, without any fear of making mistakes. Staff then provided small, portable non-permanent mark making resources: small whiteboards and blackboards, writing bats, chalks, water and brushes. Over time, children began to make marks on paper with more confidence.

Conclusion: Impact of changes to the learning environment

All the children enjoy discovering the resources in hidden areas of the garden (where they like to play). The children have enjoyed telling staff about their play.

The boys' writing projects showed that small but carefully considered changes to the environment can have an immediate impact, increasing the amount of children's spontaneous mark making and writing. This was sometimes challenging, as one project practitioner describes: *'It's hard because everything is moving and all over the place, but it's great that the children are moving around with their clipboards. And we use so much paper!'* But it was also very satisfying to see children confidently mark making for their own satisfaction, not simply at the request of an adult. All of the practitioners enjoyed the boys' enthusiastic response when they discovered new mark making resources. The boys took ownership of the resources, using them confidently and sometimes in unexpected ways as they played. In the following chapter, we see how practitioners responded to the creative expression that children show in their play and used the children's voices as provocations for creative expression in writing.

If we provide the right equipment and environment, the boys are just as capable as anyone else.

Summary: Creating a stimulating environment for writing

Keep listening to children and all the opportunities for writing with a real purpose come from that.

- Improve the quality and variety of mark making and writing resources and link them to boys' interests – make writing irresistible!
- Make sure that children can access these resources independently for most of the session
- Put mark making and writing resources in all of the areas where children choose to play, inside and outside, as well as having a stimulating writing area. Take resources to the children, rather than expecting children to go to the resources
- Create a comfortable space where children can sit on cushions or lie on the floor to write on clipboards, whiteboards or paper, as well as sitting and writing at a table
- Give children time and space to write 'on the move', to write on a large scale, to develop their gross motor skills and incorporate writing into active play
- Create a space where children can display their independent mark making and writing to show that all types of mark making are valued
- Have open-ended resources that children can use in their imaginative play to develop their oral language
- Have interesting resources and activities to help children develop the fine motor and perceptual skills needed for writing

3 Discovering a writer's voice

> On World Book Day, all of the children in a Reception class were dressed up as storybook characters. They were sitting in a circle on logs outside, getting ready to act out the story of Little Red Riding Hood, under the direction of the teacher.
>
> Teacher: *'Who wants to be Red Riding Hood's mummy?'*
>
> Ben, who was dressed as a pirate but was desperate to be involved in acting out the story, jumped up and shouted: *'ME!!'*

Quality early childhood education recognizes every child as a unique individual, full of potential and primed to learn from birth. In this chapter, we explore what this means for Early Years practitioners when they help each unique young child to discover the world of writing. We learn how project practitioners observed and listened to children as they played and we see how they used their observations of children's distinct learning styles and passions to motivate them to write. Finally, we look at some themes and practical ideas that inspire boys to express their unique voice in writing.

Building boys' confidence and motivation

Children join the 'literacy club' (Smith, 1988) by first having something they want to say – a voice – then by learning how to record that voice in conventional writing. Some children need a lot of support and encouragement before they feel empowered to express their personal voice, as they have to feel that someone is interested in what they have to say. They need adults who listen to them with interest, engage in genuine conversations and become partners in learning – quite different from the more common assessment-driven conversations that check out if children have met specific learning targets.

At the start of the projects, practitioners observed the children and talked to parents to find out about their child's interests at home. They found that many of the boys were reluctant writers, rarely choosing to write spontaneously. When they were asked to do some writing, they often said: *'I can't write'* or rushed the task so that they could go back to their play. In contrast, many of the girls chose to write, or were happy to write in an adult-led activity. In planned activities, girls were more likely to be put into the 'more able' groups and boys were more likely to be in the 'less able' groups. Claxton (2008: 18) warns us of the dangers of using children's behaviour to make judgements about their ability: *'Confusing disengagement with lack of ability is one of the most dangerous mistakes a teacher can make.'*

Observations showed that boys generally lacked the intrinsic motivation to write in an adult-directed activity but practitioners saw adult-led activities as the most effective way of teaching writing. They felt pressured to drive up attainment and this led them to emphasize the transcriptional aspects of writing over the compositional aspects, focusing on letter formation and phonics. Boys often struggled with the physical aspects of writing. In addition, if they couldn't see the point of adult-directed writing activities, they didn't engage with the compositional aspect. As they realized that they were struggling, their motivation and confidence dropped, giving them the false belief that *'If I am low ability, effort will not help'* (Claxton, 2008: 108), further undermining motivation and inhibiting learning.

Why was this? Were the boys disengaged because they lacked ability, or was the writing provision mismatched to their needs?

Writing has to be more exciting than sitting at a table.

Tickell (2011: 88–9) cites research by Dweck and Leggett (1988) and Bandura (1992), which shows that beliefs and attitudes of self-efficacy and mastery as learners are formed in early childhood. Project practitioners understood that children's self-belief and their dispositions as learners influence their ability to learn cognitively. When they observed the children in a

Discovering a writer's voice

flexible and well-resourced environment, during their self-chosen play with no prescribed outcomes, they discovered that many of the boys had a strong self-belief and were powerful learners in ways that were individual and sometimes unexpected. This was much less likely to be the case in adult-led activities.

> Sam drew a map and made it into an airplane *'so the airplane can follow the map.'*

In some cases, practitioners discovered blocks to an individual child's learning, and were able to negotiate with the child to overcome these blocks.

> We'd never thought of asking the boys why they didn't want to draw or write before. I asked Rahim if he wanted to do any writing. When he said no, I asked him what we could do that would help him want to do some writing. He said: 'I only like orange paper.' We put different colour paper on the writing table, and he did lots of mark making on just the orange paper until it ran out, then he stopped.

Practitioners wanted to harness the self-belief and creativity that they observed during self-initiated play and so they gave all children more autonomy and involvement in planning contexts for learning. Practitioners had specific curriculum targets, but they took a step back from adult-led planning and had faith that their targets could be met in ways that were inspired by the children, facilitated by the adults. They took writing to the place where children were most confident and able to express themselves, their play, discovering and creating intrinsically motivating starting points for learning that would inspire the children to write in their play.

> We're more flexible and responsive, going with the children's ideas, rather than feeling we have to get through all of our planning. It's very real for them and it frees us up to take the play on immediately rather than going away and planning.

Facilitating writing by responding to boys' styles of play

At the beginning of the projects, boys were commonly described as being physically active – 'he's an unguided missile', 'he's in perpetual motion'. They found it hard to sit and concentrate at carpet time and were reluctant to take part in writing activities at tables. Some boys were seen to be strong-willed, boisterous and competitive. Others were less confident, needing security and routines. They often enjoyed discovering and describing how things worked, and their play regularly involved listing and classifying aspects of their world. Gussin Paley (1986: 11) voices the dilemma of many Early Years practitioners: 'I vacillate between the evidence continually provided by the children's behaviour, and my need to conform to conventional standards and opinions.'

As a result of the projects, practitioners responded more confidently to this dilemma, adapting the learning environment to the needs of the boys, instead of expecting the boys to adapt to 'conventional standards'.

Responding to physical and active play

Generally, boys prefer floor play and physical play, indoors and outdoors.

Our observations showed boys racing on scooters, playing with construction, playing in garage role play outside, playing in the sand and jumping off the climbing frame.

> 'I can run very fast.' (Callum demonstrated!) 'Sometimes I call myself Sonic.'

Goddard Blythe (2005: 3) writes: '. . . physical experience is the very expression of life. Just as the brain controls the body, the body has much to teach the brain.' During early childhood, connections are established within the brain, which allow babies and young children to make sense of their world and to actively engage with their environment. The active behaviour that practitioners noted so regularly during the projects reflected children's instinctive choice of sensory-motor play activities that help them to gain the physical, perceptual and cognitive skills necessary for higher-level learning. Active play also helps children to develop the balance and control that they must have before they can sit still and perform fine motor movements needed for writing.

Initially, practitioners worried that they would lose control if they allowed boys' active style of play. Typical boys' play challenged their desire to create a calm and peaceful learning environment (Holland, 2002). But when they acknowledged the value of active play, they found that they could harness boys' spirit and energy and encourage children to mark make and write as part of their play: combining a purpose for writing with the opportunity to practice their transcriptional skills. Children were able to represent their ideas in their own personal and unique way as they played.

> A group of children were playing on bikes in their Reception class outside area, while another group of children were running round playing 'policemen'.
> Their teacher put a box of clipboards outside.
> After a few minutes, the 'policemen' sat near the bikes noting on their clipboards 'if anyone fell off a bike' or 'if they didn't tidy up.'

There was a flurry of writing - it started when we stopped doing formal planning and watched for a week.

Discovering a writer's voice

Responding to boisterous and competitive play

> Raffy and Tom were playing outside on a 'ski track'. They stood on large plastic bricks, and slid up and down, shouting: *'I'm first, I'm first!'*
>
> *Figure 3.1* Three boys are playing 'Winter Olympics'

Research by MacLure and Jones (2009) shows that classroom disciplinary practices *'that produce social order and forge a collective identity may marginalise a minority'* when children start school or pre-school. Boys can take longer to interpret and meet the expectations of a predominantly female workforce in a group setting – such as the requirement to sit still, sit 'properly', and to listen. The research also shows that, once a negative reputation has been established, it is hard to over-turn.

However, there are good developmental reasons why boys can find it hard to conform to the rules of a classroom. Testosterone is building muscle in young boys, muscle that needs to be stretched and exercised through climbing, jumping, running and throwing. Sitting still for too long is painful. High levels of testosterone can cause boisterous behaviour, and boys were

Discovering a writer's voice

often observed engaging in play fighting or 'rough housing' (Maccoby, E. in Baron-Cohen 2004). This type of play can look dangerous, but during rough and tumble play, boys are learning about self-regulation, empathy and cooperation by discovering boundaries and establishing rules of engagement. So, instead of banning play fighting, practitioners in one nursery school created a Pirate Day when children were allowed to make weapons and engage in pirate scenarios – walking the plank, capturing sailors from ships. There were no injuries and if any child was disturbed by the play, the concerns were dealt with openly and negotiations took place to make sure that everyone was safe and could join in the play. When we negotiate with children, for example when they are involved in noisy action play, they can come up with sensible solutions themselves, as Gussin Paley relates in this conversation between two boys:

> 'Use light sabers. They don't make noise. Wh-sh-sh.'
> 'No! Laser beams. That kills you really quietly.'
>
> Gussin Paley (1986: 80)

The projects showed that, when children are allowed to be active and can integrate writing into their play, inside and outside, they respond well, as one Reception teacher noted: *'When the boys are engaged in writing and mark making the environment becomes generally calmer.'*

Barney and Vinny were drawing a map showing the things they would like to have in their new Reception class outside area. They drew and wrote on a large sheet of paper on a table in the garden. Every few minutes, one of the boys stopped work and ran around the garden or climbed up the climbing frame and came down the slide. Then they went back to their activity.

The teacher helped them to label their drawings and they shared their map proudly with the rest of the class before they went home.

Discovering a writer's voice

Responding to boys' interest in how things work, in systems and classifying

Baron-Cohen (2004) attributes gender differences in behaviour that we typically observe to the existence of two different types of brain: the empathizing brain (brain type 'E') and the systemizing brain (brain type 'S'). He defines empathizing as *'the drive to identify another person's emotions and thoughts, and to respond to them with appropriate emotion'* (Baron-Cohen, 2004: 2) and systemizing as *'the drive to analyse, explore and construct a system'* (Baron-Cohen, 2004: 3). He suggests that we are all on a continuum from extreme type 'E' brains to extreme type 'S' brains, but the E type brain is essentially, and more commonly, female and the S type brain is essentially, and more commonly, male.

This is a controversial view, challenged by people who believe that gender differences are largely learnt. But project practitioners found the theory interesting and useful when they observed the boys' behaviour. Observations showed that boys often displayed an interest in understanding underlying systems when they played. They enjoyed looking at books of mazes, books that classified animals, or different types of transport, and they responded well to opportunities to write by making lists, doing surveys and making maps, drawing plans and charts and by making non-fiction books. The following observation of Toby and Harry in their Reception classroom shows their interest in knowing how things work:

> Harry: *'We're playing racers. These things push the bomb speeders off and they race along the track – watch . . . pwooooah! My bomb speeder!'*
> Toby: *'My car doesn't need that . . . it can use the ramp.'*
> Harry: *'Toby, you need something big to bomb speed, you do.'*
> Harry: *'This is a Batman mobile, it has wheels and it's a Batman car. This is his seat and this . . . He saves the world and gets baddies. Shall I tell you why he has two cars? Because if this one runs out, he speeds into this one. That car goes on the back and it speeds off. Batmobile, Batmobile!'* (he is singing). *'In case this one runs out of petrol.'*

Discovering a writer's voice

Creating opportunities for writing that inspire children

He's starting to write – but it's on his own terms.

> The Statutory Framework for the Early Years Foundation Stage (DFE, 2012) clearly states that each child's experiences, interests and stage of development must be taken into account to promote learning in appropriate ways.
>
> 1.7 Practitioners must consider the individual needs, interests, and stage of development of each child in their care, and must use this information to plan a challenging and enjoyable experience for each child in all of the areas of learning and development. (p. 6)
>
> 1.9 Practitioners must respond to each child's emerging needs and interests, guiding their development through warm, positive interaction. (p. 6)
>
> 1.10 In planning and guiding children's activities, practitioners must reflect on the different ways that children learn and reflect these in their practice. (p. 6)
>
> 2.1 (Assessment) involves practitioners observing children to understand their level of achievement, interests and learning styles, and to then shape learning experiences for each child reflecting those observations. (p. 9)

Empowering children to write

Practitioners found a variety of ways to encourage a 'can do' attitude to writing. Every setting created a display board where children could put their independent writing and mark making, including work they did at home, to share with other children and adults.

Displays were created to celebrate children's drawings, scribed comments and mark making including:

- 'I am good at . . .' Children's responses included: *sharpening pencils; watching fish; making noodles; eating ice cream; cuddling my dog; putting on my shoes*
- 'Ask me about . . .' . . .different topics, such as forest school, my favourite stories, my conker or going to the library.
- A friendship board: *'Alfie is a good friend because he helps me open my banana.'*

In some settings, children were given their own writing books to use when and how they chose – 'have a go' books, or 'special' writing books. These were

Figure 3.2 Children enjoy writing about things that they can do well

Discovering a writer's voice

very popular and more reluctant writers picked up on the enthusiasm of the prolific writers.

One Reception class established an authors' area where children's books were displayed and shared.

Open-ended and accessible resources that allow boys to express themselves in their play

Stimulating and non-prescriptive resources allow children to follow their preoccupations in their play:

> Jason was 'going on a bear hunt' as he rode his bike around the garden. He followed lines that he had drawn on a Post-it, and he pointed to places on the lines as he reached them: the forest, the swamp and the river.

> Arthur was busy making a model with boxes in his Year 1 classroom.
>
> Teacher: 'How's it going?' Arthur: 'Not very well.'
> Teacher: 'Have you got a plan, or are you working it out as you go along?'
> Arthur: 'Aaah, yes, a plan.'
>
> > He drew a plan of a 'rocket' on a piece of paper.
> > Thomas came and watched: 'Do you want any help?'
>
> Arthur: 'No.'
> Thomas: 'What are you making?'
> Arthur: 'A rocket. This is my plan sheet.'
> Thomas: 'Which bit have you made?'
> Arthur: 'This bit at the bottom. We're doing this bit. Can you hold the string please?'
>
> > The two boys worked together, holding the string, cutting, consulting the plan. Arthur: 'We're making cages for trapping the aliens! Look at our rocket! It's multi-colour!'

In both of these observations, the boys initiated the play, they were in control of how they play and they had freely accessible mark making resources that could be used to extend the play.

Planning with the children

By involving children in planning we build on children's competencies as learners, rather than putting them into a passive role as learners.

During the projects, practitioners recognized that the boys were able to take a significant degree of responsibility in their learning. They began to plan activities together that genuinely inspired the children and took their experiences and understanding as a starting point for learning.

> A group of children were planning with their teacher in an Early Years Foundation Stage Unit. The teacher asked them what they wanted to find out about dinosaurs, then she asked how they could let everyone know what they had found out. They decided they could make posters.
> The next day, the teacher said they were going to make dinosaur posters. The children all said *'YES!'* excitedly, and punched the air.

In the following observations, we can see how children learn from each other.

> A group of children in the Early Years Foundation Stage Unit were planning together around a theme of food.
> Raffy said he wanted to find out *'what people eat before they do their jobs, like in the winter Olympics they eat spaghetti.'*
> Lola wanted to find out about *'chips. To make chips you need sausages.'*
> Sophia said chips were made from potatoes: *'It is potatoes, 'cos I've seen it on the TV.'*
> Karim agreed: *'I helped my mummy do it* (make chips).'

Discovering a writer's voice

Our planning is more creative and imaginative and open-ended.

Following the boys' interests

We find activities that excite the children - not a production line. We focus more on process than product ...

Some common themes enthused the boys and these were picked up by practitioners and integrated into planned activities and responsive teaching. All of the themes combined active and physical play with mark making: writing price lists and signs, designing scoreboards for football or skittles, drawing tracks for racing cars or programmable toys, or drawing and labelling maps.

Popular starting points included:

- **Den making** – writing materials were put in a dragon's den in some bushes, and the dragon wrote letters to the children to which, of course, they had to reply.
- **Adventure themes**, such as space travel, adventure camps, spy command centres, swamps and jungles, pirates, underwater worlds, magic carpets and dinosaurs and dragons
- **Themes of 'goodies and baddies'**, adventurers and heroes, such as Robin Hood, St George, Jack the giant killer

> Ryan made a 'baddy spotter' by sticking straws onto a box: *'you look through the straws to spot the baddies and kill them.'*

- **Themes involving cooperation, competition and conflict**: races, competitive games and challenges.

> Oliver and Billy were playing with Beebots (programmable toys).
>
> Oliver: *'You're behind me, Billy.'*
> Billy: *'Yeh, but mine goes fast. Oh my god! Mine's definitely the fastest!'*

Discovering a writer's voice

> Oliver: 'Mine's going backwards – yeh, cos I want it to. Come on, come on, come on, come on! Let's have a backwards race. Yeh! I'm the winner!' He ran around chanting: 'I won, I won, I won!'

Football

> In this observation, practitioners picked up on individual children's interests to channel aimless play:
> Cody and Zak were wandering around their Reception class garden. The teacher knew that they were big football fans, so she encouraged them to play football and keep score on a chalkboard.
> They chalked: *Rooni* (Rooney) *9* and *Gerd* (Gerrard) *10*.
> Zak drew a large number 10 on a sheet of paper then he cut it out and stuck it onto the back of his sweatshirt with Sellotape.

Superheroes and special powers – often children's creativity took practitioners by surprise, as in the case of Adam, whose superhero drawing was a blank piece of paper, because his superhero's special power was invisibility!

Jobs such as builders, driving instructors, window cleaners, emergency workers and master chefs inspired creative play and language. Children made workshops and other work places such as a car wash, and a car and bicycle repair workshop where writing became part of the play.

Superheroes was the best topic we've ever done. We had huge skyscrapers going down the corridor, and lots of writing about things they don't usually get to talk about at school.

Using boys' voices to stimulate writing

Scribing has helped children see purposes for writing and they know that their writing and comments are valued. Children are more inclined to talk to adults and other children about their writing now.

49

Discovering a writer's voice

When adults scribe children's thoughts, ideas, comments and stories they create a link between oral language and writing. Scribing allows children to develop a writer's voice without being restricted by the need to form letter shapes and spell words and it helps to value their thoughts and ideas as a basis for talk for writing. Articulate children who didn't choose to write were freed up to express their ideas. Adults supported other children who needed to develop their language and communication skills, by 'recasting' and modelling correct forms of language.

As adults scribed children's words, they modelled how to write, sometimes drawing attention to letter shapes (graphemes), letter sounds (phonemes) and punctuation – while focusing on the compositional aspects of writing. Children enjoyed having their words recorded and discovered that their words could be read back and shared with other people. This helped them to discover the link between reading and writing.

> Owen, aged 3, drew a confident swathe of red lines on a piece of paper. A pre-school practitioner recorded his words, which she displayed with his drawing: *'There's no trees, trees don't be at beaches. Ummm, sometimes I fall over and the waves goes over me, but we don't have clothes on for that, we just have swimming costumes on. We go on holiday to the beach and live in a caravan. I like it at the beach.'*

Owen enjoyed hearing his words read aloud by his mother when she collected him from pre-school. The scribed words helped Owen's mother to know what the random-looking red marks meant to him.

In the same pre-school, Josh was helped to express some difficult feelings by a practitioner who helped him to make a poster:

> Josh was upset when he couldn't go outside in a heavy downpour. He drew a large, bright sun on a poster and an adult scribed his words: *'Why does it rain when we don't want it to?'*

Certain current events captured children's imagination. Raffy was excited by the Winter Olympics, which became a recurrent theme in his play. Staff in his Early Years Foundation Stage Unit helped him to create a ski track outside in the snow, and he made a book with pictures of Olympic athletes and competitions. The teacher scribed his story:

> *All of the ice skaters, snowboarders, bobsleighers and skiers had a race together on the bob sleigh track. Raffy's bobsleigh won! The ice skater came fourth and the snowboarder came third and the skiers came second and fifth.*

Storyboards with magnetic or Velcro-backed pictures gave children the chance to develop their oral storytelling skills, in English or in their first language, if they spoke English as an additional language, by re-telling or adapting well-known stories. They changed the endings, created new events, introduced new story characters or changed the setting.

Writing from role play

The boys are heavily involved in Star Wars games, and now they have moved on to making books about these games. They needed to spend weeks in role play before recording it!

Vivien Gussin Paley (1986) noticed a difference in the way that boys and girls played after telling her class the story of the *Three Little Pigs*. The girls created a 'safe' house with no chimney and no wolf, while the boys created Wolfman who comes down the chimney and boils the wolf. Children's play allows them to act out their concerns and preoccupations, each child in his or her own way.

The following stories were written after the children had spent time building dens and developing a storyline. By the time their stories were written down, they had structure, characters, pace, tension and resolution – and the two stories reflected the boys' and girls' very different styles of play.

Discovering a writer's voice

Super Boys Save the Day *(written by a group of boys)*

Once upon a time there was a team of Super Boys who lived in a base. The base was red, it had a computer with a red mouse.

The Super Boys' mission was to guard the enormous ruby that belonged to the Royal Family. The ruby was bigger than a football.

One day, the Super Nasties tried to break into the base and steal the beautiful ruby.

They tried to fight the Super Boys with their super whackers; but the Super Boys squirted gooey power at them.

'Gooey power! Gooey power! Gooey power!' shouted the Super Boys. The gooey power froze all the Super Nasties.

The Super Boys forced the Super Nasties into the King's prison.

The Super Boys and the Royal Family lived happily ever after. The End.

The Wedding *(written by a group of girls)*

Once upon a time there were seven nice, happy and excited princesses. They lived in a big stone castle on a hill that had a moat and a drawbridge too. In the garden they had a big pond and the garden was decorated for the wedding.

The princesses all had gorgeous wedding dresses and veils.

The princesses got ready in the palace, then their special limousine came to take them to church.

When they got to the old church they could hear the church bells ringing.

When the princesses were married they went to the grand reception for 340 people. They ate sausages, peas, chips, chicken nuggets, baked beans, Thai green curry chicken with rice, bacon and eggs too. The guests were looking forward to eating.

The cake was delicious and pink and had hearts on it. It had balloons around it too.

Discovering a writer's voice

> After a delectable meal the princesses went on their honeymoon to London and they went on an open top bus. They saw lots of people and houses and had an ice cream with strawberry and chocolate sauce. They had a brilliant time on their honeymoon.

Conclusion: What was the impact of listening to boys' voices?

The boys' voices that we have heard in this chapter are strong, confident, excited, bold and curious. The writing projects helped practitioners to understand and tackle inhibitors to their boys' learning and to move *'from adult planning to a child's imperative and motivation to write'* (Reception teacher). Practitioners reported that the projects were successful in creating a mastery attitude, deep level involvement in activities and children showed positive dispositions and confidence as learners. By supporting children's natural learning styles, they found that boys were playing more cooperatively, calmly and productively.

By the end of the projects there was general agreement among the practitioners that the boys believed in themselves as writers. They were keen to develop their writer's voice and they were no longer afraid to have a go at the transcriptional skills that had appeared to be so challenging. As the learning environment changed to match the needs of the boys, the boys became like 'fish in water' (Laevers, 2005).

> *He is now a true writer. He is confident in his own abilities and takes real pride in whatever he produces. This project has helped to empower him and take away the pressure that was holding him back. He has a natural ability that blossomed under the conditions we developed.*

In the following chapter, we see how children learn to express their voice as a writer when they discover the many functions and purposes of writing.

Summary: Helping children to develop a writer's voice

Overall, the project has benefited the boys by meeting their interests, giving them freedom to write without judgement, prejudice or restrictions.

- Find out what children are really interested in and the way they choose to play: observe children's self-initiated play and engage in genuine conversations with children
- Create opportunities for writing that develop from children's observed play: follow boys' interests, and create opportunities for writing based on 'real-life' experiences
- Involve children in planning for their learning
- Create opportunities that don't have a prescriptive required outcome and where children feel comfortable to 'have a go': scribe children's stories and language in play to encourage compositional aspects of writing while supporting transcriptional skills in playful contexts
- Celebrate and share all efforts at mark making and writing
- Give children time to develop their language and literacy in play.

4 Writing for a purpose

Keep listening to children and all the opportunities for writing with a real purpose come from that.

> Joshua sat under the wooden climbing frame in his Early Years Foundation Stage Unit garden. As I walked past he looked out and said: 'Who's your name? I'm Joshua, how do you do?' and he held his hand out to shake mine.

Children learn social conventions by imitating actions and behaviours that they see around them. Similarly, they learn about writing by seeing people use writing for a variety of personal and social functions and purposes (Ferreiro and Teberosky, 1982). In this chapter, we find out how Early Years practitioners can help children learn to recognize and value writing for different purposes as they play. We then investigate how writing for a purpose in play gives children the motivation and confidence to write independently and explore the conventions and properties of our writing system. Finally, we look at some inspiring writing opportunities and provocations that project practitioners provided for children.

Transforming the writing culture

> *Literacy is not just a performance skill with the written system of the language, but a cognitive tool that transforms our capacity for self-reflection, mental re-organization and evaluation.*
>
> Whitehead (2004: 131)

Writing for a purpose

As adults, we are motivated to write for numerous different reasons, from the mundane to the sublime. We write practical reminders to ourselves or we communicate feelings to someone through a note, a letter, a card or an email; we share thoughts and ideas through poetry, stories or a journal or we record a favourite recipe. All of these types of writing have one thing in common: they have a purpose that is significant to the writer and the reader. Before children become literate, they must experience the different kinds of writing that are produced in their society and culture, and then begin to create these different kinds of writing. If we want children to become motivated writers, rather than struggling or mechanical writers, we need to tune into their lives to find reasons to write that have purpose for them.

> Hector was playing with Jody in the home corner in his Reception class: *'It's nearly bonfire night! We're pretending. It's a time when we can go to bonfire night!'*
>
> Jody picked up a diary and looked carefully at a tube map: *'We didn't know where bonfire night was going to be.'*
>
> Hector came to look at the map: *'Get in our car, quickly! Let's go!'*

Observations at the beginning of the writing projects showed that boys who were identified as struggling or reluctant writers had interests and preoccupations that weren't reflected in planned literacy sessions. The challenge for practitioners was to help these boys to discover the value and purpose of writing and see that writing could help them to explore and pursue their interests further and enhance their play and learning. During the projects, practitioners and children came up with reasons to write together, reasons that had a genuine purpose for the boys.

> Mahmoud was playing in the role play shop in the Early Years Foundation Stage Unit.
>
> He wrote a sign on a piece of laminated card that said: *Bi yor iscrem her* (Buy your ice cream here) then he stuck the card onto the door of the 'shop'.

Writing for a purpose

> Andreas was digging in the sandpit, looking for treasure. A practitioner asked him if he knew where the treasure was buried. He became very excited by the idea of making a map, so he went and found some paper and pens. He drew a map and was encouraged to mark the spot where the treasure was buried with an X. Then he carried on digging.
>
> Later, he showed the map to the rest of the class, and in the afternoon there was a flurry of map making among the children, led by Andreas.

Whitehead (2004) reminds us that the word 'writing' is both a *verb* – a process of creating written text – and a *noun* – an end product, a piece of writing. The recent preoccupation with summative assessment in the EYFS has placed the emphasis on writing as a finished product over the process of writing as a way of communicating thoughts, feelings and ideas. A focus on the finished product directs practitioners' attention towards transcriptional aspects of handwriting, spelling and presentation, which require a didactic teaching and learning approach. A focus on the *process* of writing allows a creative learning and teaching approach that mirrors the way young children learn, and both builds on their competencies and understanding and becomes a tool that aids future learning.

Writing for a purpose in play

Knowledge and skills stay indexed according to when and how and why you learned it.

Claxton (2008: 85)

At home, children see functional writing in a range of everyday contexts, in a comfortable and relaxed environment. However, observations showed that, when boys were asked to write in their Early Years setting, they viewed writing as a formal 'school' activity that had little purpose for them, and which had little connection with their play or their interests. They enjoyed learning about forces (physics) by using pulleys to carry the Lighthouse Keeper's lunch and they had fun learning about the properties of materials (chemistry) by making

Writing for a purpose

pizzas, but they were picking up a message that writing wasn't relevant to their lives. Many of the boys already believed that they couldn't write.

During the projects, practitioners set out to challenge the boys' lack of interest, self-belief and motivation. They created playful representations of real-life reasons to write which helped children to make links between the world of writing (which they might see at home) and their own experience. Focusing on the communicative aspects of writing freed children up to 'have a go', as the purpose of the writing (a verb) was to convey a message, which enhanced their play. Many of the children, particularly the boys, couldn't see the point of doing a piece of writing (a noun) simply for the teacher.

> A role play pizza restaurant had been set up in a class of Year 1 and 2 children. The play was becoming rather noisy and boisterous.
> The teacher reminded the children that a visit from the Health and Safety inspector was due, who might shut down the restaurant if she found pizza boxes on the floor and a messy kitchen.
> The children scurried around filling in Health and Safety forms and writing in the complaints book as they tidied up, before settling down to play customers, waiters and chefs in the restaurant.

Writing became just as much fun as making pizza when it had a purpose and was part of their free-flow play (Bruce, 1997). The project practitioners found that they could 'plant' ideas for writing that helped children develop their play, such as making an officer's badge when they were playing policemen, or tickets for a puppet show, making road signs or number plates, or writing pirate messages in bottles. Practitioners modelled and demonstrated the conventions of different types of writing in context, as well as modelling transcriptional skills. The children were able to learn, apply and practise the conventions of spelling and punctuation when writing was a part of their playful learning experience, in a well-resourced and flexible environment where they were inspired to create writing that had meaning for them individually. They quickly started to come up with their own reasons to write in their play.

Writing for a purpose

> Two children are playing pirates outside. Liam has a plastic bottle with a 'note' inside, on which there are some letter shapes, then random marks, then letter shapes. Alex demonstrates that he knows the difference between letters and letter-like marks.
>
> Liam: 'It's a message in a bottle.'
> Alex: 'Shall I get it out?'
> Liam: 'It's says, "blah, blah, blah, blah . . ."'
> Alex: 'No, it says "walk the plank . . . and scribble . . . and fight."'

Writing and mark making is natural, it's a part of life.

Exploring and mastering the writing system

Very young children imitate the whole act of writing alongside a responsive adult who assists in the collaborative construction of meaning. Long before they understand the phonetic system needed to create readable text, children will mimic the writer's pose, fill whole pages with writing-like marks, give meaning to their marks and ask an adult to read their 'writing'. They do this as part of their play.

Bruce (1997) defines three stages that children move through in a 'progression in play' and we can identify these stages when children write.

Stage 1: Exploring and experimenting – what is it? Children begin by making random marks on different types of paper and other materials, with different mark making tools. Their explorations can be self-motivated but are also influenced by the availability of interesting resources and the responses of people around them.

Stage 2: Representing – what does it do? Children make letter-like marks and letter shapes on materials such as small books, postcards, tickets or diaries. They understand that the marks are a symbolic representation when they give meaning to their marks or ask an adult what they have written.

Stage 3: Free flow play – what can I make it do? Children now use their mark making and writing as part of their play, using a ticket to go on a train journey, or making a hospital appointment in a diary.

> *The role of our earliest writing partners . . . is as significant as that of our first conversational partners.*
>
> Whitehead (2004: 153)

Children progress through the stages as they experiment with mark making and writing in their play. They are likely to move easily into the role of a writer if they see positive models of people writing and if they see print attached to situations and objects that relate directly to their lives and interests, such as logos for sweets or cereal, the Play button on the DVD player, or their name card. Adults can help them by commenting on their writing and recognizing when children are ready to learn the mechanics of writing: that certain symbols can be combined to create words that convey meaning, and that particular conventions are used in different kinds of writing. If they are given encouragement and support, children will be able to practice, develop and refine their transcriptional skills of writing. But we must give them the opportunity to develop their writing skills through play, exploration, active learning and critical thinking (DFE, 2012) just as with other areas of learning.

Discovering the properties of writing

When children learn to speak, they identify grammatical rules that they apply logically and increasingly accurately as they get to know the idiosyncrasies of the English language. Adults encourage children to experiment and refine their spoken language by engaging in conversations and modelling the correct forms of language – not through instructional teaching. A two year old who says 'I goed' will naturally self-correct before long if she repeatedly hears the correct form of the language.

Written language mirrors aspects of oral language, but it has a permanence and consistency that allows children to explore and learn about the system, just as they can explore and learn about physical objects, once they have grasped the concept of letter–sound correspondence (Bissex, 1980: 285). When they understand that symbols can represent sounds, children should be encouraged to write independently and purposefully in an emotionally safe environment so that they can explore the phonological rules that make up our written system.

Writing for a purpose

> The children in a Reception class painted self-portraits and labelled their paintings.
>
> Mallee wrote: *'I hav brn her. I have brn is. Mallee'* (I have brown hair, I have brown eyes)
>
> Charlie wrote: *'blools blondher Charlie'* (Blue eyes blond hair)
>
> *Figure 4.1* Children labelled their self-portraits

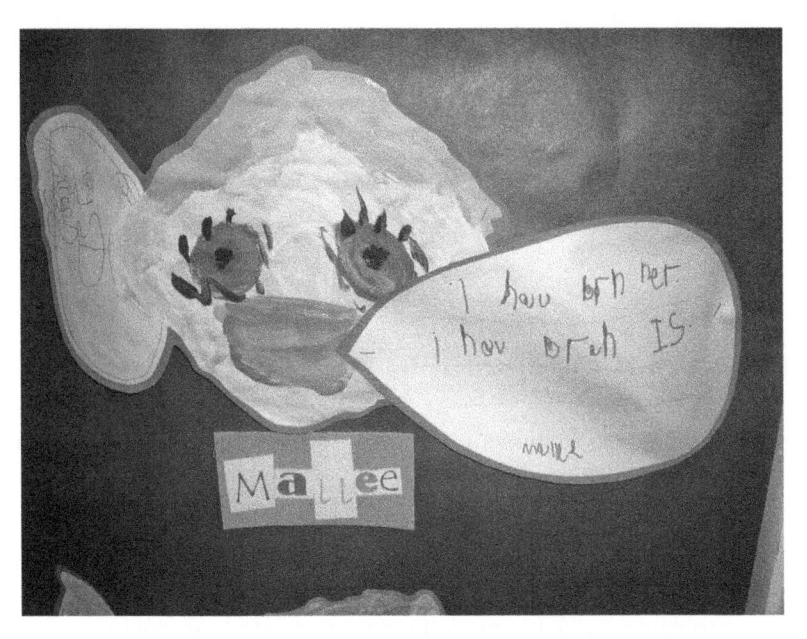

Children need to be taught our phonics system and have support resources such as alphabet strips to allow them to be independent when they write. But then, like Mallee and Charlie, they need lots and lots of practice. If we ask children like Troy and Max, below, to copy write, we transmit a message that there is a correct way to spell that they haven't learnt yet and this can inhibit children from having a go at writing. Copy writing stops children from testing and developing their own understanding.

Writing for a purpose

> Troy and Max were asked to write labels for different parts of the body and glue the labels onto a worksheet on which an outline of a person had been drawn.
>
> Troy copied the word *hand* and glued the label onto his worksheet. 'This is boring, isn't it?'
>
> Max: 'Yeh, it's boring, isn't it?'

Max and Troy's level of involvement was very low (Laevers, 2005). They didn't engage with the activity, as it had no challenge or intrinsic purpose for them. Telling a child something is the least effective way of ensuring that learning takes place.

The value of independent writing

When children write independently, they often use a system of invented spelling based on the sounds that they articulate. Encouraging children to speak their messages supports this approach. Their independent writing shows us their level of understanding and this allows practitioners to plan appropriate learning experiences. There are many research studies that show that children have no problem moving from independent spelling to conventional spelling (Bissex, 1980).

Independent writing allows children to express themselves and communicate their own messages:

> *Cep off ar nest* (Keep off our nest)
> *I menit im gointoo et you up!* (I mean it. I'm going to eat you up!)

Independent writing encourages a 'can do' mastery attitude:

> Tom wanted to know how to spell a word and was about to go and find a dictionary when he stopped and said: *'I know, I'll just have to work it out.'*

Bruner believed that teaching involves framing any subject content in a way that fits the child's way of viewing things, and this depends on the child's stage of understanding. Complex fundamental ideas are taught initially at a simplified level, and revisited in increasingly complex forms in what he called 'the spiral curriculum.'

> *We begin with the hypothesis that any subject can be taught effectively in some intellectually honest form to any child at any stage of development.*
>
> Bruner (1977: 33)

One pre-school practitioner discovered during the project that children are capable of taking more responsibility for their own learning than she had realized, and she and her staff changed the way they worked with the children.

> *We listen to them more and we don't keep questioning them. The most revolutionary thing was when we stopped correcting them.*

This practitioner wasn't advocating that adults should stop teaching correct ways of writing, but she stopped focusing on children's mistakes. Instead, practitioners observed and built on the level of skills and understanding of writing that children demonstrated in their independent play, when they were at their most able. They understood that teaching should take place within a child's 'zone of proximal development' (Vygotsky, 1978) helping them to build up their personal 'learning power' (Claxton, 2005). It should help children to build on what they can already do, rather than focusing on what they can't do. Instructional teaching was kept to short adult-led activities and children were given plenty of time to apply, practise and consolidate the newly learnt skills.

Writing for a purpose

> Learning should not only take us somewhere, it should allow us later to go further more easily.
>
> Bruner (1977: 17)

> *The children are writing at their own level in their play. It makes their play more interesting, it gives it more scope.*

> *Children are motivated in phonics sessions because they see a purpose for learning sounds.*

Creating opportunities to write for different purposes

> *We noticed that children were more motivated to write when there was a real purpose.*

During the projects, practitioners came up with creative ideas for writing for many different purposes and children were constantly seen mark making and writing in all areas of the provision, inside and outside.

Becoming an author

Children developed their writing individually and collaboratively. Some of the writing was recorded with the help of an adult scribe, while some children wrote independently and their work was shared in carpet sessions and displayed in the book corner and on the wall. They wrote stories about exciting themes such as dragons, pirates and superheroes and they made information books, following up their own particular interests or as part of a class focus; they wrote poems and spells; and they made diaries and photo books of activities and outings. Simple ideas, such as adding speech bubbles to drawings and photos, inspired a number of boys to develop their stories.

Writing for a purpose

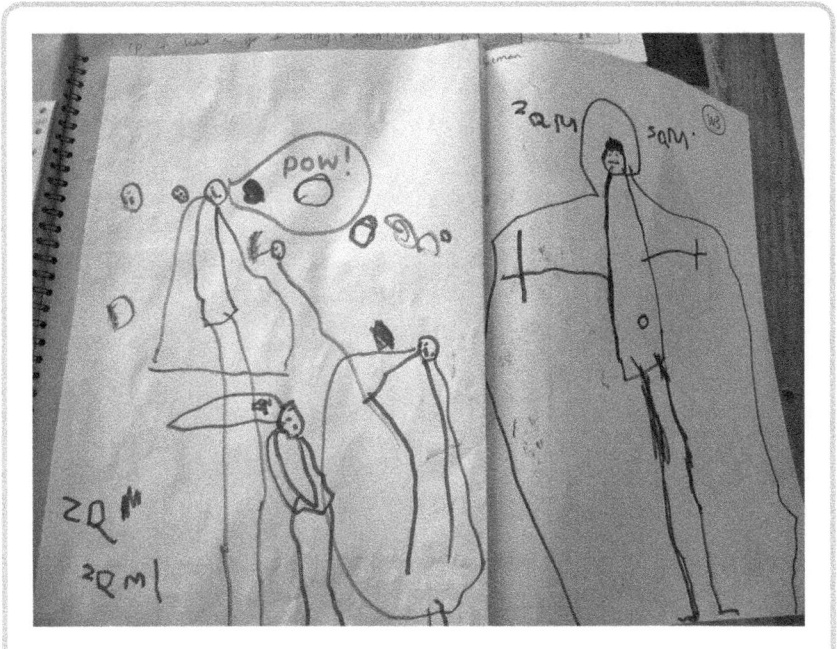

Figure 4.2 Sam's writing took off when he started adding speech bubbles to his drawings

Children also became authors by creating spoken narratives and alternative worlds in their role play, in small world play and with their models. They enjoyed using computer animation and digital photography to record their ideas.

A group of Years 1 boys were enjoying making Mobilo model transformers. They created characters and described the characteristics of their models.

'The armpits turn into guns to shoot the bad guys. They're baddy transformers.'

Their teacher gave them large sheets of paper and they made drawings of planets and bases for their models.

'Mine comes from Bangolia.' 'Mine is Forest.'

continued

Writing for a purpose

Figure 4.3 Children developed complex stories based on their model making

A Year 1 class made an animated movie of the story of *Tiddalick the Very Thirsty Frog*. They made small plasticine models and took hundreds of photos of the models in very slightly different poses to make a few seconds of film.

'I've found a way to Disneyland. Come on guys, this is the way to Disneyland, come on!' William ran off, and two other boys followed him . . .

Other innovations that stimulated children's oral storytelling included creating a storyteller's chair and making an outdoor stage.

Writing for a purpose

Writing to friends and family

Children wrote to friends, family, visitors and invented characters. Sometimes this was as part of a dialogue, for example when a group of children wrote a letter to a visiting librarian and he replied. Sometimes there was no expectation of a reply, when they sent a birthday card or invitation. Children wrote:

- Postcards, birthday cards, seasonal cards, party invitations, reminders and notes
- Messages and notes on a friendship board, on a 'Leave me a message' boards and in message boxes
- Invitations to their family to come to special events at their setting
- Messages in bottles to pirates
- They also sent oral messages using talking tins, walkie-talkies and mobiles.

Classroom organization and writing in the environment

The boys race outside to write their names on the chalk board list, to take their turn to write their own number plate for the bikes.

Writing in the environment often has the function of creating order in potentially chaotic situations – for example, road signs control traffic flow, other types of signs and labels tell people where to go in public spaces. When these forms of writing were introduced into children's play, it enhanced the quality of play and made it more collaborative and constructive.

> Two boys were playing 'prisons' in a noisy and disruptive way in their Early Years Foundation Stage Unit. They were encouraged to create a prison in an area of the classroom by writing a 'prison' sign. This transformed the play, which developed a narrative storyline.
>
> In the same EYFSU, children made road signs and number plates for the vehicles. The play moved from individual children riding aimlessly around on the bikes, to more social and interactive play.

Writing for a purpose

Children wrote their names on:

- Laminated sheets, next to photos of dressing up clothes when it was their turn to wear them
- Lists of children who were having packed lunch or school dinners and self-registration sheets
- Lists for taking turns on the computer or the bikes
- Place labels for lunch
- 'Well done' certificates, to celebrate their work.

They made signs and labels for the classroom:

Cum and mac a dinosor (Come and make a dinosaur)
Keedorb, compoot, mous (Keyboard, computer, mouse)

Children contributed to planning webs, and they negotiated rules, which were written up and displayed.

Writing in role play

Writing frames to support role play were very popular and encouraged previously reluctant writers to 'have a go'. Some children made writing-like marks, others included letter shapes and some children used their phonic knowledge as they moved towards conventional spelling. Adults supported the play, by modelling how the writing frames could be used. Children enjoyed writing:

- Appointment cards, complaints books, Health and Safety forms, tickets, forms, MOT certificates, car service records, road signs and number plates, menus, shopping lists and more . . .
- Stories as varied as *Peter Pan*, *The Gruffalo*, *Mr. Gumpy's Outing*, *Jack and the Beanstalk*, *The Three Billy Goats Gruff* and *Percy the Park Keeper* inspired story writing, letters (*Dear Giant, I'm sorry I took your golden harp*), posters (*Wanted: Captain Cook*), signs (*Beware of the Troll*) and more . . .

Writing for a purpose

> Children created Santa's grotto in the corner of their pre-school room. They made gift tags, cards, labels for presents, posters, signs and they wrote letters to Santa.

Sharing information and instructions

Children understood that writing was a way of sharing information when they used drawings and writing to record recipes for cooking, instructions for making play dough or planting seeds (*'They're special kinds of sticks, they tell us what plants they're going to grow into.'*) and when they filled in service manuals and repair logs during their role play.

> Ivan was sitting on 'space ship' made of hollow blocks outside, making marks like cursive writing on a clipboard.
> 'That means we have to fix our space ship. Don't let anyone fix it. We have a shiny one. We put the plugs inside them. We have to clean it up, we have to make it shiny.'

They made:

- Treasure maps, maps of the universe, large maps chalked on the ground outside
- Posters and leaflets
- Newspapers and magazines
- Price lists
- Children made planning sheets for their models and they wrote labels when they displayed them
- They made surveys (*Have you seen an alien?*) and recorded data about the birthdays of the children in the group, about their eye and hair colour, about experiments and investigations, such as information about size of their sunflowers.

Writing for a purpose

Reasons to write that link with children's fascinations

Space explorations, superhero missions and pirate expeditions became more satisfying when there were maps and plans to follow, when children made lists of equipment to take on their explorations and when they could relay messages home in special 'space capsules'. Children began to make links between their oral language and writing as they played.

> He loved it when he found a whiteboard in the pirate ship. He wrote 'help the baddies are coming'.

> He regularly looks for pen and paper to use in play for messages and missions.

Children wrote:

- Space log sheets
- Police reports about the robber in the garden
- Lists of jobs for the car repair workshop
- A superhero wristband
- A license to fight naughty pirates
- Labels – shark jam, weevil biscuits, pirate ship names
- Weather charts
- A list of jobs for pirates – swabbing the deck, mending the rigging – and a repair schedule for the ship
- A recipe for salami ice cream!
- Football club logos and footballers' names on their shirts (or names and logos for superheroes, or astronauts . . .)
- A letter to the giant
- Prices and signs for the car wash
- Signs, prices, order forms and architects' plans for the builder's yard
- A list of supplies for space voyages or for spy missions
- Tickets for the race track with seat numbers
- START and FINISH signs for races

Writing for a purpose

- Customized 'racing cars' with labels and logos on the handle bars
- Lists of the drivers' names in winning order, and rosettes for the winners
- I spy books.

> Liam is writing on a diary in the home corner. He sits in a relaxed posture, with one leg across his lap balancing the diary on his leg, holding a mobile phone to his ear, under his chin.
>
> 'Yes . . . no . . . that's ok . . . yeah, good, good. Ok.'
>
> He makes writing-like marks in his diary. When the phone call is finished he places the phone in his back pocket, puts the pencil behind his ear and the diary under his arm.

> Shaun and Rory are lying on their tummies in the book corner looking at a 'top secret' notebook. They find a 'special' pen and start to draw and write letters.

> Henry is playing in his Reception Class garden: 'Just have to get something for the dragon's den.'
>
> He runs to the writing trolley to get a writing bag.
>
> 'This is my dragon sack. It's got glue, chalks, scissors.'

Music, songs and rhymes

Music was used as a prompt for mark making, talking and writing in many of the settings. One nursery class listened to nursery rhymes while the children drew pictures on a long roll of paper. Another class listened to

Louis Armstrong's *A Wonderful World*, which stimulated lots of discussion and creative mark making and writing.

Conclusion

Adults have to be able to write if they are to function well in their work and in their personal life. During the projects, many of the boys discovered this imperative for themselves, and found that writing helped their play unfold, as practitioners helped children to use writing for real purposes: to discover new facts, to create and use gadgets and machines and to explore, navigate and try out different worlds.

As children spent more time writing, practitioners became better at assessing children's level of writing development and scaffolding their learning within their zone of proximal development (Vygotsky, 1978). In the following chapter, we will explore the role of the adult in supporting and extending children's writing and mark making in more detail.

Summary: Creating conditions where children have genuine purposes for writing

We now have boys writing in corners, corridors, outside, inside, through role play, construction ...

- Observe children's play, tune in and respond by 'planting' writing resources or ideas that contribute to the play – then move away
- Plan real-life contexts that give children a genuine compulsion to write
- Model purposes for writing and encourage children to write for different audiences
- Always encourage children to write or mark make for themselves to allow them to construct and refine their own understanding of the writing system
- Make sure that writing resources are available in all areas of provision, inside and outside, so that children don't miss the moment!

- Scribe for reluctant writers to allow them to create and convey meaning without having the pressure of transcribing their writing. Encourage them to add their name or a few words if possible (such as *Love from*, or *To*).

5 | The role of the adult in supporting young writers

Learning and teaching should not stand on opposite banks and just watch the river flow by; instead, they should embark together on a journey down the water. Through an active, reciprocal exchange, teaching can strengthen learning how to learn.

Loris Malaguzzi (n.d.)

When project practitioners were asked 'what have you done that has helped boys to become writers during the project?' they gave some interesting and wide-ranging responses. They talked about having *'high expectations but putting less pressure on children'*; they said that the children were secure and knew that *'the adults genuinely care'*; they talked about *'observing children'*, *'empowering children'*, and *'valuing everything from the earliest mark making to conventional writing'*.

We take it a step further now.

In this chapter, we explore the multi-faceted role of the Early Years practitioner in supporting children's positive learning dispositions as well as teaching writing skills. We find out how practitioners can help children to co-construct their learning within a 'negotiated classroom'. We see how the ORIM framework (Hannon, 1995[E2]) can support practitioners as they help children to become confident writers. Finally, we consider the place of handwriting in the context of early writing development.

The complex role of the Early Years practitioner

How did practitioners take 'a step further'?

Taking a step further meant that first practitioners took a step back. They looked at their practice with fresh eyes, drawing on their observations and knowledge of the sociocultural backgrounds of individual children and their knowledge of child development. They challenged their own assumptions about individual children and groups of children and questioned their own value system.

Socially constructed learning

The developmental theories of Lev Vygotsky and Jerome Bruner underpin the 'social constructivist' approach that has been at the centre of much inspirational Early Childhood education around the world. Both Vygotsky and Bruner observed that children's learning takes place in a social context with adults and more experienced peers, who model and guide children's learning using a process known as scaffolding. Their work built on that of Piaget, who identified set stages in children's development – and took it further.

> *Teaching does not wait upon development but propels it.*
> Smith (1993: 56), quoted in Fisher (1996: 32)

Scaffolding requires the teacher (or parent or other involved adult) to have good knowledge of the child's stage of development, level of understanding and interests. The adult helps to move the child's learning on from their *Zone of Actual Development* ('what the child can do alone today') by supporting them in their *Zone of Proximal Development* ('what the child can do with assistance'), during familiar routines or situations that engage the child (Vygotsky, 1978). This can only happen when adults spend time observing and getting to know their children, and reflect on their own practice.

The belief that children actively construct their learning with support from adults isn't new. John Dewey wrote in 1897:

> *The child's own instincts and powers furnish the material and give the starting point for all education. Without insight into the psychological structure and activities of the individual, the educative process will . . .*

> be haphazard and arbitrary. If it chances to coincide with the child's activity it will get a leverage; if it does not, it will result in friction, or disintegration, or arrest of the child nature.
>
> Dewey (1897: 77–80)

The plural practitioner

Rose and Rogers (2012) acknowledge the complex role of adults working with young children by proposing seven key dimensions that define the 'plural practitioner'. The first of the seven dimensions is that of 'critical reflector' and practitioners took on this dimension wholeheartedly through the course of the projects.

> *By articulating their implicit belief system, by carefully examining any pre-judgements, practitioners are more likely to develop a pedagogic role that is finely tuned into children's needs and interests and encompasses more proactive expectations of children's learning potential.*
>
> Rose and Rogers (2012: 30–1)

Practitioners reflected on how they took on the other six dimensions of Carer, Communicator, Facilitator, Observer, Assessor and Creator. They aimed to develop nurturing relationships that enhanced children's holistic development; to become the 'guide by their side' (Rose and Rogers 2012: 84); to make assessment an integral part of their day to day practice; and to create spaces where children had genuine choices about *how* they learn, while the practitioners guided *what* they learnt.

> *At a whole school staff meeting we explained about the project and the EYFS. A Y4 teacher said, 'You do all that?!' in total surprise. It raised the status of the EYFS in the school and other teachers' understanding.*

The adult as facilitator

> . . . in guided play teachers enhance children's exploration and learning by commenting on children's discoveries; by co-playing along with the

children; through asking open-ended questions about what children are finding; or exploring the materials in ways that children might not have thought to do.

Fisher et al. (2011: 6)

Project practitioners set up an enabling environment with stimulating and open-ended resources that encouraged children's motivation to write spontaneously in their play. But the resources alone weren't enough. Skilled adults were crucial in scaffolding children's learning by modelling how children could use resources, supporting them to find reasons to write that moved their play on, motivating and enthusing children to want to write, and teaching transcriptional skills at appropriate times. Adults needed to become *Creators* of learning spaces and opportunities and *Facilitators* of learning (Rose and Rogers, 2012).

In a genuinely enabling learning environment, practitioners respect children's agenda and encourage children to be protagonists in their learning.

> Charlie was making a model in his playgroup. He chose to make his model from a light bulb box *'in case there's a power cut.'*

They consider carefully if their own agenda is more important than that of the child. They negotiate with children when possible, and explain why a child's personal agenda sometimes isn't possible, as children develop an understanding of social expectations.

Personally I stepped back and spent a lot more time watching and listening. This felt like a luxury but it's integral to all of us as Foundation Stage practitioners. Blocking out 'external' pressures was difficult but it has paid off, with boys becoming writers from the 'inside out' rather than the 'outside in'.

The negotiated classroom

Very young children learn by observing, copying, testing out new hypotheses and adapting their ideas in response to their experiences – all very effective learning strategies. Why should this change when they start in formal educational settings? Gussin Paley recognized that children quickly learn that teachers make unilateral decisions and accept this. 'This is unfortunate, because our best thinking – mine and theirs – often emerges from our biggest disagreements' (Gussin Paley, 1986: 28).

The concept of the 'negotiated classroom' challenges 'the myth that being a pupil is different from being a child' (Fisher, 1996: 109). It challenges the view of the pupil as the recipient of learning determined by the teacher, and promotes the notion of the child as a competent learner from birth. Learning becomes a 'wandering spiral' (Edwards et al., 1998) where adults and children interact and co-explore ideas, revisiting learning with deeper understanding over time; where adults provoke new ways of thinking and teach skills or help children consolidate learnt skills in their play. The adults understand the potential for learning in play, and they plan for specific learning, but children share responsibility as to how learning is achieved. Often, the learning will go in unexpected directions and emerge at unexpected times, and no cap is set on the learning, as can often happen when teaching is target driven.

Negotiating with children gives them a sense of ownership over their learning environment. One Reception teacher found that giving up break times had a big impact by increasing the time for free-flow play, inside and outside. *'Children have more time for continuous in-depth activity, thus extending their learning and adults' opportunities for observation.'* When lunchtime came, it was hard to pry children away from their activities!

Learning and development become a 'process of transformation through people's participation rather than of acquisition' (Rogoff, in Podmore and Luff, 2012[E4]: 24), whereby adults and children engage in joint problem solving and active co-construction of learning. Practitioners resisted the pressure to 'cover' a curriculum, and focused on helping children to 'uncover' the learning (Katz, 2011).

> *It's almost as if you're taking a step back and enjoying it with them, rather than having your teacher hat on all the time.*

Creating shared expectations

Children need consistent boundaries and expectations from adults within a negotiated classroom and children *'are more likely to "risk" new things if they*

The role of the adult in supporting young writers

have a sense of adult support' (Nutbrown[E5], 1994: 32). These boundaries need to be made clear: in particular, it appears, for young boys who need to be introduced to classroom systems and expectations more explicitly than girls.

> The context was a Reception classroom, where some children were having their snack at a table and others were involved in their play. A girl was sitting on the floor by a table crying and Danny was standing nearby holding a chair, looking confused and worried. The teacher helped the girl up and comforted her then took the boy aside and gently asked him what had happened.
>
> This is the series of events that had taken place:
>
> - When the children had started in the Reception class they were all told to sit down at the snack table when they wanted some fruit and a drink
> - One day, Danny went to the table and couldn't find a chair to sit on, so he stood and waited
> - The teacher told him that he could take a chair from another table if there wasn't one free
> - So that's what he did on this occasion . . . but he didn't realize that the chair belonged to May who was reaching across the table for something, only to find that her chair had gone when she tried to sit down – so she went bump on the floor, and started crying.

A practitioner with a strong type of 'empathizing' brain (Baron-Cohen, 2004) might tune into the emotions of the situation ('How do you think May felt when you took her chair?') rather than the underlying systems that Danny needed to understand. This teacher wisely listened to the facts, then she explained the system to Danny: next time he needed a chair he should check that no one was using it before he took it. Problem solved, Danny went off a little wiser and better able to function in the class situation.

Much of the print we see around us every day is there to create common expectations, a sense of common purpose and to give us information that we need to enjoy being part of a community: road signs, parking regulations, bus timetables, signs telling us not to drop litter, or to keep our dog on a lead,

The role of the adult in supporting young writers

posters advertising films, menu boards outside cafes to entice us inside. When we reproduce these types of writing in an Early Years setting, we help children to develop a sense of their place in the community, as well as an understanding of why we write, and at the same time we can motivate them to write and encourage them to share their writing publicly.

> **Tidying up:** one EYFS unit tackled the issue of tidying up by encouraging children to take ownership of certain jobs. Each child made a poster and these were put up in the appropriate area of the classroom: *My jod is wellis.* (My job is wellies).
>
> **Classroom rules**: these can be negotiated, agreed and written with children. This can be made more interesting by, for example, writing rules for superheroes in the classroom!
>
> **Play fighting:** when weapon play spills over into aggression, children can apply for a gun licence. They explain why they need a 'gun' and agree to use their weapon according to negotiated rules. Their reasons are recorded on the licence.

Figure 5.1 Making posters for the classroom

The role of the adult in supporting young writers

> **Turn taking:** Aidan wanted to go on a bike in his pre-school garden. An adult suggested he wrote a letter to Ewan, who was riding on the bike, asking if he could have a go. He did, and Ewan immediately gave him a turn.
>
> In another setting, children made number plates for the bikes. They wrote their name on a whiteboard under the number of the bike that they wanted to ride.

When the boys are engaged in writing or mark making the environment becomes generally calmer.

The role of the adult: What does it look like in practice?

Whitehead (2004) explains how formal adult-led literacy activities are simply the tip of the 'literacy iceberg'. Beneath the tip of the iceberg lie the crucial experiences of sharing stories and nursery rhymes, seeing adults model being a writer and seeing print in the environment. These experiences are 'invisible' to the extent that one parent whose child, Charlie, was an avid book-lover by his first birthday, believed that she had 'done nothing' to support her child. In fact, she had been reading to him from birth, cuddling up and sharing books in an emotionally safe and comforting environment.

The ORIM model

The ORIM model (Hannon, 1995[E7]) was developed as a framework to support parents' involvement in their child's early literacy development, to make explicit some of the 'literacy iceberg' that is submerged and unseen. This framework can equally be applied to the role of the Early Years practitioner.

The model recognizes that children need:

- *Opportunities* to write
- *Recognition* from an adult that their mark making constitutes early writing and their oral language constitutes 'storying' and adult *recognition* of the child's stage of development in writing
- *Interaction* by an adult to encourage, support and scaffold children's literacy learning
- *Modelling* by an adult of writing in context.

Opportunities – resources and time

In Chapter 2, we saw how project practitioners created an environment full of *opportunities* for writing. As practitioners spent more time observing children, supporting child-initiated play and encouraging mark making and writing everywhere, they recognized that routines were likely to break up play and learning, and that their expectations of times and places where writing should take place were too narrow, too formal and were often chosen by adults. Once they discovered that boys liked to mark make and write in the context of their play, some practitioners increased opportunities for writing by changing the organization of the day to allow more time for extended free-flow play. Children were able to play together and pick up on each other's interests in a less structured environment.

> Lewis made a badge, supported by an adult scribe, on which was written: *Lewis, sheriff 4*. Maia wanted to make a badge too, and she wrote *Sajunt 5* (Sergeant 5) on her badge.

We found that giving children time, not cluttered with too many group sessions, resulted in more independent writing.

Recognition – tuning in to the boys

We decided to take the risk of being more child-led, to loosen control.

Practitioners became better at recognizing the children's individual voices in their mark making.

> A child in a pre-school made marks on paper that initially looked random. His key person recognized that two parallel vertical lines represented a tree trunk and three horizontal parallel lines represented the lines on an inflatable boat. The drawings were put into a book with photos of the objects that they represented, and the book was shared with the child and his parents.

Some settings developed their team work, supporting all practitioners to recognize the potential for writing in children's play by creating and displaying lists of ideas for writing in all areas of the continuous provision to extend children's play.

Interaction

Practitioners acknowledged that it could be problematic when boys' play became noisy and boisterous, but intervention to channel play productively can be difficult to achieve.

> Three boys are making models with small construction in their Reception Class.
>
> Finn: 'Mine's a double light sabre.' (He breaks his long model in half.)
>   'See? Two light sabres, you can use whichever you want.'
> Andrew: 'I've got 2 guns, because Finn's a baddy. He's got a big gun.'
> Felix: 'Baddies always have big guns.'

continued

The role of the adult in supporting young writers

> Felix and Andrew go under the table and make shooting noises at Finn who waves and spins his light sabre.
> Felix and Andrew 'shoot' Finn.
> Finn: 'No, I'm on your team now.'
> They dive under the table, shooting with their guns, dodging and spinning their light sabres.
> Their teacher sees the boisterous play and comes over: 'How about playing a different game? You could make a space ship.' Finn pulls a miserable face and his whole body slumps.
> Teacher: 'Have you got a space ship?'
> Andrew: 'Who in the world would be foolish enough to do that?'
> Teacher: 'Do what?'
> Andrew: 'Go into space.'
> Teacher: 'But I thought Star Wars was in space?'
> Andrew looks confused and walks away. A few minutes later he made a model. 'Look, look at my space ship. This is the shooting bit.'
> Felix: 'We don't have shooting, remember. Mrs Hibbert said.'

Supporting learning in child-initiated play is a complex skill. When practitioners connect with children's play, they can guide them towards specific learning by suggesting ways to take the play forward, by offering resources, or by making a passing comment. This can motivate, inspire and support powerful learning, as long as adults don't try and dominate children's play, as the following observations show.

> Some boys in a Reception class were enjoying rolling cars down a piece of guttering with gusto, but several of the cars smashed when they reached the ground. The teacher described how, before taking part in the project, she would have told the boys that she would take the cars away if they couldn't be more careful.
> Instead, she suggested that they might like to build a car repair workshop. She provided real bricks, sand, water and buckets and the boys worked together enthusiastically to build a structure. At the end

of the morning, they realized that the older children in the school were going to walk past and they were concerned their structure might get damaged.

George suggested that he could write a sign. He went and found a laminated sheet of paper and a felt pen and settled down to write on a bench by his car repair workshop. The teacher asked him if he needed some help and George, who until now had refused to write, said 'I can do it.'

He wrote: Ddc me dow (Don't knock me down) and he put his sign in front of his building, confident in the belief that he had written a sign that other children could read.

Figure 5.2 George made a sign as part of his play

continued

The role of the adult in supporting young writers

> Some children had created a 'train station' outside. A practitioner asked where the train was coming in. When Barney said the train was coming in to Platform 2, she suggested that he made a platform sign, so she would know where to go. Barney became very excited and he wrote a large number 2 on a piece of card and they found a way to stick it on the wall. William said they needed a Platform 1 and Platform 3 sign, which the two children made and displayed.

We focus more on process than product, our planning isn't so elaborate.

Practitioners found imaginative ways to enthuse boys to write, ranging from picking up on children's interests as they played to planning specific activities, drawing on observations.

> Acting out familiar stories:
>
> Children in an EYFS unit acted out the story of *The Enormous Turnip*, taking turns to try and pull the 'turnip' up while their teacher narrated the story and the children joined in with repeated phrases. Later, they made individual and collaborative books and the children acted out the story independently with the props. They used small world figures, storyboards and story sacks to re-tell the story orally.

> A group of boys in a pre-school were playing with cars when an adult gave them a road mat. She quickly realized that the road mat stopped them from making their own roads, so she took it away and put large sheets of paper down instead. The boys then drew their own road network, drawing on their knowledge of the local area.

Figure 5.3 Writing labels

After reading the story of *Dear Zoo*, children planned their own zoos and made models of animals in boxes, with labels on them.

Our planning is more creative and imaginative and open-ended.

Other planned and responsive ideas for writing, mark making and the oral creation of a narrative included:

- Videoing children's play and watching the video together
- Creating a 'storyteller's chair', tent or willow arbour
- Performing a play, and making tickets and posters
- Writing instructions for making light sabres
- Writing licences for guns or light sabres
- Writing in a Health and Safety book for a space ship
- Taking photos and making a slide show on the computer, with a written commentary
- Using film-making software to make a short animated film with plasticine models (I Can Animate).

The role of the adult in supporting young writers

We stopped being so prescriptive about where and when and more importantly how writing might be done.

We're now confident enough to let them do lots of independent stuff, without feeling we have to bring them in and do something structured.

We're seeing less 'come over here and do this for me' and more supporting play. It's a slow process but it's happening.

Modelling

Adult modelling of writing behaviour gave children a purpose for their writing and the celebration and 'publishing' of children's work gave them the incentive to write.

Practitioners joined in with role play, extending children's narratives. They modelled the *process* of writing and they modelled different *purposes* for writing, which children took into their play.

> Frank, age 3 years, was playing in the role play building site in his pre-school when his key person joined him.
>
> She asked: *'Back in your office?'*
> Frank: *'Yeh.'*
> Adult: *'Have you got any appointments today?'*
> Frank answered: *'Work.'* He picked up a brick to use as a telephone and spoke with a deep voice: *'Got to order it in. My car broke down. It's got a hole and broke its wheels. You got to order it in. Or out. You do it. Me going in my office. Me got to do my work.'*
> Adult: *'Well, I'll order the cement then.'* She picked up a 'phone'. *'What time will it be here?'*
> Frank: *'18, 13'*. He put a straw in his mouth, then ordered sweets and cigarettes on the brick phone.
>
> Later – he used a brick to scan his mark making *'Doooooooooooo dooooooo dooooooo doooo.'*

More children are using role play areas, and their play is better after adults model writing behaviour.

> At group time, the teacher showed the class some of the children's writing, commenting: *'I really like the way you write the words under each other. That's how we write a list,'* and she reminded the children that they had written lists that morning in a teacher-led activity.

> The Reception class teacher talked to the class about making surveys, asking them what they would like to find out. Together, the class made a survey to find out who had been to the library. The teacher modelled a way of recording the survey on a large whiteboard.
>
> During the free-flow play, some of the children chose to make their own surveys on small portable whiteboards. They drew a chart with two columns, with headings *Yes* and *No* and they asked other children questions relating to their survey. One child chose to ask 'who's seen an alien?'

Practitioners modelled giving value to writing, by sharing and celebrating children's work and by documenting the learning process with photos and commentary. When children saw their independent writing or scribed writing displayed on an author's table or on the wall, they learnt that books are created by authors and that authors are people just like themselves.

We now make more of an effort to tell them when we're writing, like: 'I'm just going to write a reminder that Owen is going to Mason's house today.'

Teaching transcriptional writing skills

The writing projects aimed to build children's confidence and motivation as writers, and so the main focus was on the process of writing, on developing a

The role of the adult in supporting young writers

writer's voice and understanding different purposes for writing, as we have seen in Chapters 3 and 4. But practitioners also wanted to raise attainment, and they explicitly taught writing skills in meaningful contexts, using methods appropriate to the age and developmental stage of the children. Children were introduced to phonic work and transcriptional skills were demonstrated in short planned activities. Practitioners then modelled and facilitated children's writing in contexts that helped children to apply the taught skills. As children came to write more confidently in their play, practitioners found that *'children are motivated in phonics sessions because they see a purpose for learning sounds'*.

Phonics teaching helps children to become independent writers, once they have made the giant leap in understanding to recognize that writing is a symbolic system and that letter shapes represent oral sounds. Just as we read books to young children that are beyond their independent reading skills so that they can enjoy and be inspired by wonderful stories, it is crucial that adults continue to scribe for children after they begin to write independently, so that they can use language creatively at a level beyond their transcriptional skills. As they scribe, adults can sometimes draw attention to spellings, punctuation or letter formation appropriate to each child's stage of writing development, if they can do so without breaking the child's creative flow.

Teaching handwriting

Handwriting is a physical skill, distinct from the compositional skills that children need to learn before they can communicate in writing. Handwriting ultimately needs to be legible and presentable but the physical act of writing can be a struggle for young writers who are still developing their physical strength and coordination. Overemphasis on handwriting at too early an age is likely to damage children's motivation to write as they struggle to make the small, precise movements required to write neatly.

Project practitioners gave children abundant opportunities to develop hand–eye coordination and practice the gross and fine motor control that would help them to refine their handwriting skills. Children, especially the boys, loved writing on large and small chalkboards, whiteboards and gel boards, in non-judgemental contexts, rubbing out their marks and starting again, or making marks in gloop and with finger paints. They made marks on interactive whiteboards and on large sheets of paper, using whole arm movements and smaller wrist movements. They made marks with chalks, large brushes and paint or water outside, and they developed their upper body strength by climbing and swinging from bars. Practitioners modelled correct letter formation when they wrote in contexts that interested children, and they supported children to practise writing letter shapes by providing resources, reasons and encouragement to write.

> *Movement is a child's first language and is the building block to enable a child to physically write.*

Conclusion

During the course of the writing projects, the role of the adult shifted significantly. Less time was spent on adult-led, decontextualized teaching and, instead, practitioners spent more time motivating and inspiring children to become expressive and creative writers. Practitioners' enthusiasm was contagious and children absorbed positive messages about writing and were able to meet curriculum targets for writing in enjoyable, self-initiated, purposeful play.

Children learnt that writing is useful; that writing is fun; that writing is part of everyday life; that writing is non-threatening; and that everyone can be a writer.

Practitioners were reminded that becoming a writer is just one facet of children's holistic development. The vast mass of the 'literacy iceberg', of which formal writing is just the tip, consists of children's personal, social and emotional well-being, and their physical, language and creative development. In the next chapter, we see how writing became an integral part of all aspects of provision, and supported all curriculum areas.

> **Summary: The role of the adult in supporting writing**
>
> *I've taken a step back, and am scaffolding their learning. One thing leads to another ... you observe, find out what children really know, and build it into your planning.*

The role of the adult in supporting young writers

- Set up an enabling environment with open-ended, stimulating mark making and writing resources, and time and space for children's deep-level learning
- Model ways of using writing resources in contexts that have meaning for children
- Tune in to children's preoccupations and interests; pick up on children's intentionality and respond sensitively to support writing in play
- Plan mark making and writing activities based on observed interests
- Plan with the children
- Support compositional aspects of writing by prompting and listening to children's thoughts and ideas. Help children to record their thoughts and ideas by scribing their words and by providing video and voice recorders
- Teach transcriptional skills by modelling being a writer, by teaching the symbolic system explicitly in planned activities and by reminding children to apply their knowledge in their independent writing
- Motivate and inspire!

6 | Writing and cross-curricular learning

In previous chapters we have seen how the boys' writing projects supported all children, boys and girls, to become writers, helping them to develop both compositional and transcriptional skills as they made connections between writing and all other curriculum areas. In this chapter, we explore how writing skills become embedded when children have opportunities to practise writing in cross-curricular learning, and we see how cross-curricular learning is supported by children's developing writing skills.

Young children's learning and development doesn't happen in compartmentalized curriculum areas. Their developing oral and written language gives them an increasingly sophisticated cognitive tool with which they can make human sense of all aspects of the world around them (Vygotsky, 1962) and extend their knowledge and understanding. They explore important questions: 'who am I?' and 'what can I do?' so that they can take their place in the world with confidence. They learn to communicate with others and express their curiosity, their wonder, their anxieties, their investigations and their discoveries. They develop a sense of self in space and time, using all of their senses to investigate and manipulate the world. They discover and use numbers and patterns. They learn how they can represent their ideas in a 'hundred languages' (Edwards et al., 1998).

Effective learning happens in real-world contexts through playing and exploring, active learning and creating and thinking critically (DFE, 2012). Piagetian theory sees play as a means of unifying experience, knowledge and understanding, and this was evident when children were encouraged to write in play experiences.

Writing and cross-curricular learning

> *Children can learn more than adults can . . . Play turns out to be among the most deeply functional human activities.*
>
> Gopnik (2009: 73)

Making connections across the curriculum

At the beginning of the projects, most of the writing in the Early Years settings took place with an adult in prescribed activities with specific literacy objectives, usually at tables. Resources and opportunities were provided elsewhere, but only a few children, mostly girls, accessed these independently. Boys were generally reluctant to write with an adult at a table, and, as a consequence, were often identified as 'low ability' writers. However, they were keen to initiate and follow their own play agenda, and this became an asset when child-initiated play was used as a starting point for learning rather than something that happened, unsupported by an adult, after 'real' learning had taken place.

When children have high involvement levels, learning takes place at a deeper level (Laevers, 2005). Open-ended play opportunities allow children to follow their individual interests and these will be different for every child and will encompass all learning areas. In the following observation, Albi and Aaron are making connections in their learning as they follow their own play agenda, drawing on the story of *The Gruffalo* to enhance their play.

Two boys are sweeping up sand by the sandpit, when an adult comments that the marks in the sand look like monster tracks.

Albi: 'There are monsters in every classroom. They've got . . . BLACK EYES! And prickles all over them! And sharp, sharp . . . nails. Claws. They eat everything, even when they're not hungry.
I SAW ONE!'

Aaron: 'You know who the monsters are? Us! My mummy says "you cheeky monster!"'

The offered curriculum and the received curriculum

We can stimulate and guide children's learning, but in the event they will focus on what's important, interesting and significant to them at the time.
de Boo (1999), quoted in de Boo (2004: 11)

Planning (the offered curriculum) has an important place in Early Years settings, to make sure that children have varied opportunities to develop their confidence and enrich their thinking and learning in a broad and balanced curriculum. But however carefully practitioners plan, we know that children will take selectively from the experiences that they are offered (the received curriculum). The only way we can know what children are 'receiving' from the curriculum is by observing them in unstructured situations.

Young children need a balance of adult-led learning (with specific learning objectives), adult-initiated learning (with potential learning identified by the adult, but children can follow individual lines of enquiry) and child-initiated learning opportunities (Fisher, 1996). During the projects, practitioners found that they could shift the balance of their planning towards more adult-initiated and child-initiated learning. This gave them more time to observe how children were receiving the curriculum and to support them as they explored and discovered how things work, identifying, labelling and classifying their discoveries and imposing order on the world, using writing to enhance their learning. When practitioners become facilitators of learning (Rose and Rogers, 2012) they can teach specific skills to children in their play, when children are more likely to 'receive' the teaching.

In pre-schools in Reggio Emilia in Italy, 'provocations' are provided in the form of ideas and resources, to stimulate interest and encourage exploratory learning without any predefined expected outcome. Reggio practitioners talk of the thousand possible responses that their planning might provoke, knowing that children are likely to come up with the thousand and first response. Many of the possible responses can include mark making and writing, but very few of them will be solely literacy focused. Learning will inevitably cross curriculum boundaries in ways that might be predictable but which often go in entirely unexpected directions!

Writing and cross-curricular learning

> A group of pre-school boys found a large cardboard box. After a short discussion, they used the box to create a 'sauna'.
>
> In this observation, the cross-curricular learning that took place included:
>
> - **Science and technology**: children discussed the temperature of the sauna and how to make it hotter and colder (adding a temperature control)
> - **Geography:** they discussed different places where they had seen saunas
> - **Literacy**: an adult scribed their messages on signs: *Danger HOT* and *open* and *closed*
> - **Literacy** and **mathematics:** an adult scribed on a sign: *3 children allowed* and a child drew three people
> - **Physical development:** of fine and gross motor skills
> - **Social and communication** skills
> - **Expressive arts and design**
>
>   . . . and more!

By the end of the writing projects, children were discovering the relevance and the power of writing, and many of them were writing *'anywhere, anytime'* in contexts that encompassed science, mathematics and other curriculum areas. Every time they wrote or an adult scribed for them, they made a connection between writing and reading, recognizing that their writing could be read by others, and that they could read other people's writing. Writing in play helped children to understand that there are conventions of spelling and grammar and that they need to learn these conventions so that other people can read their writing.

Creating opportunities for writing in all curriculum areas

We discovered from our observations that mark making needed to be encouraged and facilitated throughout the curriculum.

The writing projects supported learning in the Prime and Specific areas of the Early Years Foundation Stage (DFE, 2012).

Links between the prime areas and writing

Personal, social and emotional development

A crucial aspect of early literacy development is personal autonomy – the clear establishment of a sense of control over one's learning experiences.
Evangelou et al. (2009: 35)

Children in the Early Years are developing a sense of self. A Danish pedagogue, working with 4-, 5- and 6-year-olds in a Copenhagen kindergarten explained that her priority was for children to know *'This is who I am'* so that they can start school with a strong sense of self: as an individual, within a group. In England, we place high emphasis on literacy skills in equipping children for school. The writing projects showed that a focus on children's personal, social and emotional development can support children's literacy learning – helping them to form strong relationships with adults and other children, establishing positive dispositions and confidence as learners and acquiring self-regulation as they develop the motivation to write. How did this happen?

Collaborative writing and mark making took away fear of the blank piece of paper and allowed children who were reluctant to write to make a confident contribution in their own way, at their own level. Children made group books, contributing ideas while practitioners scribed. They drew and wrote on large pieces of paper on the floor, on tables or on walls. They wrote and made marks on whiteboards and blackboards, enjoying rubbing out and making more marks. They created stories over days and weeks, drawing on paper and making puppets, culminating in a performance for parents when 'every child has a chance to shine'.

Children were given 'have a go' writing books, where they could experiment with writing at any time. They wrote in home-made books expressing their personal interests.

Writing and cross-curricular learning

> Joe's Book (scribed by his nursery teacher)
>
> That is a map of the world.
> That is a mouse.
> That is a mountain.
> This is a road crossing each other.

> Tom, aged 4 years, made an Animal Magazine at home and brought it into his nursery to show the staff and children. It had a drawing of a free gift of a ruler on the front cover and his mother scribed the words on each page.
>
> p. 1 The hunters killed many more things than the tigers in the olden days.
> p. 2 A poster
> p. 3 A tiger for you to colour in
> p. 4 Join the dots to make a tiger

These activities allowed children to focus on the *process* of writing and they moved towards conventional writing at a comfortable pace, with sensitive adult support. Books, independently written or scribed by an adult, were displayed in 'authors' areas' and independent writing from home or the early years setting was displayed on 'We can write' boards. Displaying and sharing writing with friends and family helped to establish positive attitudes to writing.

As children become more confident, willing and able to rise to challenges, they establish and embed beliefs and attitudes that support self-efficacy and self-regulation (Bandura, 1992 in Tickell, 2012: 88).

Some ways of promoting children's personal, social and emotional development through writing

- Self-registration
- Turn-taking lists for popular activities
- Den making in groups with signs and maps

Writing and cross-curricular learning

Figure 6.1 Children found their names for the self-registration board

- Make a list of class rules
- Make 'choice boards' with pictures and written labels of resources to help children make choices
- Make a visual timetable with written labels to help children deal with transitions
- Create a friendship board or tree where children can post messages
- Make message boxes for every child where they can give and receive messages, special gifts, invitations, cards etc.
- Make personalized books about children's families, holidays, achievements and preferences
- Involve children in planning and setting up resources and areas of learning
- Use Persona Dolls to explore issues that cause children anxiety and help develop empathy. Display the dolls' life stories and write letters
- Write letters and cards for special occasions or when someone is ill or on holiday.

Communication and language

Developing story language, functional and descriptive language

During the projects, oral language development was seen as a priority and a prerequisite for children to become confident early writers. Children have to be able to talk a message before they write it; they need to be able to hold thoughts in their head and express them orally using increasingly complex grammatical constructions, and a wide functional and creative vocabulary. Project practitioners devised different ways to support children's speech, language and communication skills.

Children were encouraged to enjoy books by talking about the pictures, relating stories to their own experiences, joining in with story language and playing around with stories, making up alternative endings. Storytelling chairs, dens and tents were set up inside and outside, where children went independently to make up and share stories. Storytelling projects helped children to develop a framework for writing stories and gave them specific story language so that they were well equipped to create their own stories as they developed transcriptional writing skills (Corbett, 2010).

Group activities and circle times were planned to support the development of language skills that would enrich children's writing. Pirate play offered plenty of opportunities for children to use skills such as hypothesizing, articulating ideas, listening to other people's views and revising their own ideas. They negotiated an agreement that they could only have weapons if they had a pirate weapon licence showing that they could use them safely, and the licence would be revoked if weapons were used inappropriately. They discussed the roles and responsibilities of different pirate crew. They created pirate menus to prevent scurvy, and made a 'spare parts' shop, selling peg legs, parrot food, binoculars and other essentials for pirates (all labelled).

Some children enjoyed using 'talking tins' to record messages, which encouraged compositional language.

Children developed their vocabulary alongside adults, experimenting with materials that stimulated their senses. They described sounds, textures, tastes, smells and visual stimuli as they explored textured and scented play dough, feely bags, drinking chocolate finger paint, went on sound walks and tried new and unusual food.

Writing and cross-curricular learning

Language for thinking and expressing ideas

> Max, aged 4 years, is playing with diggers in a sand tray on the floor of his Reception classroom. He talks to the practitioner as he plays.
>
> *'I like covering him* (the digger) *and then he sinks, cos it's sinking sand. You just take one step in there and then you sink, like he's sinking, and you can't see his light.'*
>
> A digger is lying on its side in the sand. Max covers up the digger's light with sand.
>
> *'That guy's in the sand, he's just crashed. When I get back tomorrow the whole thing is going to sink. That's going to sink. Those bits can't be sank, they go down. You can't see them, can you?'*
>
> He tries to cover up part of a large digger with sand.
>
> *'It's hard to get the big wheel done. This digger doesn't sink. He's been good. I'm going to sink his light and see if it can light when it's been covered. It CAN light when it's been covered!'* He laughs excitedly.

This observation of Max gives us a window into the process of his thinking and his understanding as he shares his fascinations by giving a commentary as he plays. We see that he uses language to communicate with the adult who is at the sand tray with him, and to help him to think aloud and move his understanding on. The fact that he is thinking aloud allows us to discover that he enjoys drama and action and to learn that he is a systemizer, as he explores concepts of size, mass and weight (Baron-Cohen, 2004).

Simple provision of sand and diggers captured Max's interest, and stimulated his exploratory language and thinking. Practitioners can help children to develop their language and communication skills by engaging with them in their play, commenting and speculating or asking a few open or supportive questions to help children to extend their thinking. They can also introduce specific resources or 'plant' ideas to take children's learning on a step.

Max's self-initiated play could be used sensitively to allow him to make links between oral language and purposeful writing.

- A practitioner might suggest to Max that he makes a sign for the sand tray saying, *DANGER, sinking sand*

Writing and cross-curricular learning

- He might prefer to make a map, showing the location of the sinking sand, so that engineers and architects can build roads and houses away from danger areas. He could draw and write on large sheets of paper, and use small blocks and cars
- He might choose to draw a picture of the diggers in the sand or take a photograph and tell an adult about his play while the adult scribes his words in a home-made book or on drawing paper.

The writing projects don't just relate to writing things down on paper, but also it's about investigating different materials so that, when they move the magnets over the iron filings they can see what happens to them and describe what is happening.

Physical development

Observations in all of the project settings showed that boys need to be on the move but this conflicted with expectations for behaviour during literacy activities, particularly in schools. Sally Goddard Blythe explains how the development of the vestibular system – knowing 'your place in space' — receives its training through movement. Children need to experience movement to learn 'the art of not moving' (Goddard Blythe, 2005: 12) before they can sit at a table and write for any length of time.

Reading and writing require directional awareness, and writing depends on hand–eye coordination, skills that are developed by moving the body through space, vertically, horizontally, forwards and backwards and spiralling. Keeping children at tables until they have finished a formal piece of writing is counterproductive. When we allow children to move in and out of action and static writing, they find their own rhythm, self-regulation and motivation.

During a visit to Early Years settings in Finland, a group of Early Years practitioners found that mats were provided so that children could choose to write lying on the floor. Project practitioners confirmed that the boys' preference (and sometimes the girls') was to write on clipboards or on large sheets of paper lying on the floor inside or stretched out on the grass, and they rarely chose to come to mark making activities at tables.

Some ideas for supporting fine and gross motor development and writing

- Make writers' toolkits, belts, backpacks or lunchboxes for children to write 'on the move' inside and outside
- Provide clipboards and large sheets of paper for children to write wherever they feel comfortable
- Develop descriptive and positional vocabulary by attaching language to dance and movement – twirling, swirling, slithering, above, inside, under – and write poems or draw diagrams of mechanisms with moving parts
- Provide resources for children to develop fine motor skills needed for handwriting, such as screwdrivers, locks and keys
- Forest School offers wide-ranging opportunities for learning in all curriculum areas.

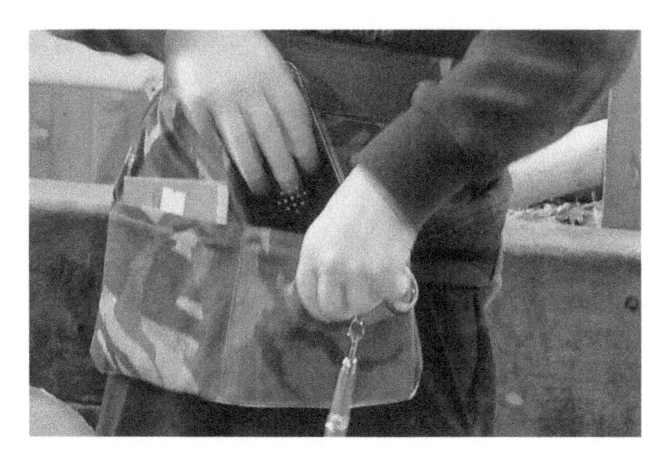

Figure 6.2 Writing belts encouraged children to write in their play

'I like going to forest school when it's raining. I stick out my tongue and catch raindrops.'

One boy says he 'needs his writing on the move bag' when we go for walks!

Links between specific areas of learning and development and writing

Mathematics

Children learnt that mark making and writing are important in many everyday contexts as they developed their mathematical understanding.

They learnt the difference between number symbols and letter symbols when they made birthday cards for people of different ages and as they wrote page numbers on home-made books.

They linked writing and numbers in role play, for example, writing price labels and using a shop till, writing shoe and clothes size labels, and using calendars and timetables.

They learnt about numerals as labels when they wrote and recognized number plates for wheeled vehicles and in numbered parking bays. They learnt and wrote their own house numbers and made calls on mobile phones.

They learnt how to record quantity as they kept score in games by tallying or writing numerals. They helped adults to write signs such as: *3 children allowed in the sand* and they made surveys and charts.

They learnt about ordinal numbers when they made medals for first, second and third place in the 'Winter Olympics' races, and as they raced programmable robots.

Number rhymes and songs helped children to explore the rhythm, pattern and pulse of language. Explicit links were made with writing through song books and cards, and when children made their own books, maps and pictures to illustrate number songs and rhymes.

Books such as *Katie Morag Delivers the Mail* or *The Jolly Postman* can be used to prompt children to write and post letters, matching words and numbers on their letters with different addresses.

Most importantly, all mathematical activities had a purpose that linked to children's interests. Children who had a special football team wrote the names and shirt numbers of their favourite players. They helped make birthday charts and height charts in adult-led activities.

The following play scenario demonstrates how one boy reflected his developing mathematical learning in his play. He has learnt some number names and knows that symbols on a tape measure represent numbers, but hasn't yet learnt to match symbols and numbers accurately.

> Barney was playing outside in his pre-school.
> *'There's a sign on there.'* He pointed to the 'bus stop' sign on the shed door and then he started measuring the wall with long tape. A practitioner held the top end and asked what number was at the bottom, just as another practitioner walked by saying, *'It's twenty to twelve, it really is time to tidy up.'*
> Barney looked at the tape and said *'20, 12.'* He measured another wall and said the number was *'20 o'clock.'*

Understanding the world

Children discover that *'they can use marks to help them to make sense of their world, to solve problems or discover solutions to their lines of enquiry'* (The National Strategies Early Years, 2008: 3).

Children learn that writing is a valuable tool alongside experienced adults, as they explore their physical world and as they learn about the passing of time and discover diverse ways of living as a family, keeping traditions and celebrating special events.

People and communities

Exploring the world through real visits or imagined journeys offers scope for different types of writing. During the projects, children enjoyed drawing maps, bringing mark making and geography into their imaginative play as they charted their space travel or plotted pirate voyages showing where treasure was buried. Children went for walks in the local area and they drew maps of the route to their Early Years setting. They made maps of the route that a colony of ants took from under the log pile to the crack in the paving slab on the path.

They visited the country of dragons and the world of kings, queens and knights. They found special writing materials in dragons' dens (*'Follow the dragon's footprints!'*) and wrote letters to the dragon. They made books about themselves, a short time ago, when they were babies and toddlers. They found out what life was like a long time ago for servants, kings and queens who lived in castles.

Writing and cross-curricular learning

The world

Boys' play often revolves around the use of tools, appliances and technology, as we see in this observation of Lenny, as he rides his bike in the Reception class garden.

> Lenny passes a traffic cone and calls out to an adult: *'It's a speed camera, to stop cars going superfast.'*
>
> The practitioner asks him how it works.
>
> *'You press this button and then you spy how fast people goes. That's how we do it. No one spies on us, 'cos we spy on them.'*

Observations such as these led to the provision of opportunities for mark making and writing that supported boys' fascinations. They became architects and engineers, drawing plans for new bridges and houses, zoos and adventure playgrounds. They became 'spies', and recorded things they spotted in special notebooks. They became botanists, lepidopterists, entomologists, ornithologists and zoologists, enjoying the sound of these special words and taking pride in hunting for rare and special wildlife. They learnt that it was important to record and classify their findings – some real and some created in their imaginations – on charts and in books.

They built hides, and watched for birds through binoculars. Sometimes the hides would turn into camps and dens for commandoes, superheroes, pirates, princes or dinosaur hunters.

They planted seeds and bulbs and wrote labels to record the name of the plant, their own name and the date. They drew charts to plot the growth of their plant.

A microscope connected to a computer encouraged careful observation and discussion, and findings were recorded on paper or on the computer.

Children also used marks spontaneously to explore their understanding of the world as in these observations of Leon, who is learning about volcanoes, and Paul, who is exploring thoughts and feelings about night time.

Writing and cross-curricular learning

> Leon, aged 3, is drawing spots and 'splats' on paper with thick felt pens. He explains: *'this is the flames . . .* (the splats) *They come out of the volcanoes'* (the spots).
>
> Paul is drawing at a table. He drew lots of black swirls and said:
>
> *'I'm just going to put some black bits here – to make it scary. It's the middle of the night.'*

Technology

One practitioner harnessed two boys' fascination with technology to encourage writing in their play. She helped them set up a race for programmable floor robots. The boys drew a target on a large sheet of paper, and set the robots to move towards the target. They drew marks and wrote their names showing where the robots stopped and recording which robot had won the competition.

Figure 6.3 A classroom display shows how a group of children made an animated film

Writing and cross-curricular learning

A Year 1 class read the story of *Tiddalick the Frog* and made short animated films based on the story, using plasticine models. The boys' transcriptional skills showed a significant improvement when they wrote the story after creating the animation.

Many of the boys were motivated to mark make and write on whiteboards when they were allowed to photocopy their whiteboards. Others wrote labels for their models when they wanted to leave them out on a display shelf.

Some ideas for supporting children's understanding of the world through writing

- Make passports for real or imaginary journeys
- Create a favourite character, such as Charlie Bear, who can go home with the children. Children can write about the visit in a special diary with drawings or photographs
- Write recipe books and menus for food from a range of cultures and countries, throughout the year (not just as celebration of a specific festival)
- Give children a small video camera to make recordings, which can be put onto a computer with added text. Children can watch the videos on a laptop or interactive whiteboard
- Digital cameras can be used to take photos during an activity or a visit, and put onto a computer or printed out to make books or displays with explanatory text
- Explore environmental print by making timetables, road signs, TV guides, instructions for appliances, open/closed signs and signs showing shop opening hours.

Expressive arts and design

The Hundred Languages

The child is made of one hundred.
The child has
a hundred languages
a hundred hands
a hundred thoughts
a hundred ways of thinking
of playing, of speaking.

Extract from *The Hundred Languages* by
Loris Malaguzzi (Edwards et al., 1998))

Writing and cross-curricular learning

Children explore feelings, thoughts and ideas in their play using different forms of symbolic representation. Writing is one important means of expression but an environment that recognizes children's 'hundred languages' values the power and creative voice of children such as Casey. The following observation demonstrates how creative children can be when they are given time and space to follow their ideas, and when we adapt the learning environment to the children, rather than expecting children to adapt to the environment. Casey's model was totally unique – one that would never be found on a planning sheet written by an adult!

> Casey made a model from cardboard tubes, straws and material and announced proudly that he had made *'a pair of swim protect engine swim slide mud binoculars, with paddles to help the binoculars go in water and material to protect the engine'*.

Figure 6.4 Casey's model

109

Writing and cross-curricular learning

Writing can be used to capture children's creativity, when adults scribe children's language while they draw or make models, dance or create music, to reflect the ideas and thinking that lie behind different symbolic representations.

Some ideas for supporting expressive arts and design and writing

- Create performance areas for drama, circus skills, dancing to different types of music or puppet shows. Make posters and tickets for shows
- Provide props to enable children to take on the role of characters from favourite stories
- Create a mark making and colour mixing shed, den or open space outside with paint palettes and rolls of paper, small and large blackboards and whiteboards for mark making
- Put wallpaper up where children can draw design ideas, for example, in the construction area and for den building
- Write labels for models
- Sing songs and make music that encourages 'musical conversations': call and response chants, copy a musical pattern
- Create musical routines such as welcome and goodbye songs, and songs or musical cues for tidy up time
- Sing action songs and play around with songs, changing the words and adding new verses.

Conclusion

We have had a complete rethink of the way we encourage boys to use the mark making facilities. We follow the ideas and preferences of the children, helping us to provide learning experiences best suited to all our children and helping us to recognize the best way to develop our boys' mark making and writing skills.

In New Zealand the Early Years curriculum, Te Whariki, is based on the idea of a woven mat, where practitioners weave strands comprising *'all the talents and dispositions of young children together with the areas of learning considered important by their society'* (David 1999: 10). Learning to read and write is essential in literate societies, and in England, in contrast with New Zealand, the EYFS places high store on developing formal literacy skills as part of the 'school readiness' agenda. However, the *'qualities and skills that are most valued by schools, the ability to communicate orally and represent ideas on paper, are often the very aspects of learning that boys find most difficult'* (Primary National Strategy, 2007). The projects showed that learning to write doesn't have to be difficult when cross-curricular contexts are created that allow children to develop writing skills alongside other important areas of learning.

Children start to build up the 'roots' of literacy (Goodman, 1986) from a very early age, when they see members of their family engaged in everyday, functional literacy at home. In the following chapter, we see how developing a partnership with parents can allow children to build on their informal home literacy experiences when they move to an Early Years setting.

> **Summary: Helping boys to become writers through cross-curricular learning**
>
> *We take the writing to the boys, rather than expecting it to be the other way round.*
>
> - Observe boys when they are playing, to see what they are 'receiving' from the 'offered' curriculum
> - Provide real-life play experiences with versatile open-ended resources that allow boys to make meaningful connections within and between all areas of learning during their free-flow play
> - Support boys' interests by taking writing to their play. Don't expect them to stop playing so that they can write at table
> - Don't make judgements about boys' writing abilities based only on their performance in adult-led activities, as this can damage boys' self-esteem and confidence in themselves as learners
> - Plan opportunities and provide resources where boys can develop the fine and gross motor skills that will allow them to become writers
> - Model how writing can support boys' mathematical, technological and scientific enquiry
> - Tune in to boys' creativity – it might be less immediately visible than that of the girls. Give them opportunities to express themselves through a wide variety of media
> - Trust that *all* children are naturally powerful and competent learners, curious to explore and make sense of their world.

7 Working with parents to support early writing

In previous chapters we explored how children's literacy development can be enhanced and supported in the context of Early Years settings. Research shows that parental involvement in their children's early literacy experiences is key to children's later social and academic success. Early Years settings have an important role to play in creating respectful relationships with families and in supporting parents' confidence and understanding of their role as early educators (Siraj-Blatchford et al., 2011). In this chapter we consider the literacy experiences that take place in the first few years at home, creating the conditions that allow children to learn to read and write. We explore ways to establish a strong partnership between Early Years settings and parents that take account of all children's home cultures and experiences. Finally, we look at some practical ways to create a partnership with parents that builds on their strengths as educators at home, allowing young children to take more from their pre-school experience.

The roots of literacy

Just as babies need to hear language and be involved in conversational interactions before they learn to speak, children need early literacy experiences before they can become writers. Children's literacy development begins as soon as parents and other important people in a child's life read to them, sing songs together, read the words on a cereal box or write a birthday card or a shopping list. As children observe and take part in these everyday simple and fun activities, they begin to understand functional literacy in a relaxed context and they develop the 'roots of literacy' (Goodman, 1986).

Children gradually become aware of the physical form of print in contexts that have meaning for them – for example, seeing their name on birthday cards or recognizing the name of their favourite biscuits in the supermarket. They discover the difference between words and pictures as they enjoy looking at books, listening to stories and talking about the pictures with a caring adult. They learn the oral language used to talk about written language when they sing alphabet songs and when adults point out 'words' that have the 'letters' in their name. They absorb conventions such as styles of writing for different purposes and discover that writing is directed at an unseen audience when the childminder reads an email that their mother has sent them from work.

These 'roots of literacy' (Goodman, 1986) need fertile soil in which to grow. The best place for this to happen is in a natural and often unconscious way at home – for example, by drawing in steam on the kitchen window, singing songs at bath time or writing text messages or reminders to phone the doctor. These spontaneous literacy activities happen in the context of caring, secure relationships, fulfilling a fundamental psychological need for learning to take place through supportive human interactions (Bruner, 1977).

The National Writing Project (1989) describes some important experiences for early writers that form the fertile soil. Children learn about writing by having a variety of non-fiction and fiction books, including songs, rhymes and poems, freely available to look at alone or to read with others. They might have access to a cosy space with beanbags and a low bookcase, or more simply, a box of favourite books within reach of a crawling baby or toddler. They might have lots of books of their own, or they might enjoy a trip to the library to borrow books.

Children learn from caring adults who draw attention to print all around them, on the computer, on posters, labels and road signs: a parent might talk to their child about a notice that gives the opening times for the swimming pool, a poster advertising the fair or the 'no dogs' sign in the local park.

They learn by seeing adults or older children who provide positive models of writers: for example, when a parent reads an email from granny to the child, or writes a comment about a cousin's Facebook photo. Adults contribute a significant element of the fertile soil when they give children lots of encouragement to draw and write in an unpressured environment.

The importance of the home environment in early literacy development

The Effective Provision of Pre-School, Primary and Secondary Education (EPPSE 3–16) project explored the different contributions of family, pre-school and school to children's social and educational development. Key findings (Siraj-Blatchford et al., 2011) from this longitudinal study suggest why and when some children 'succeed against the odds' while other children, from both disadvantaged and 'privileged' backgrounds, fall behind.

Quality home learning environments

> . . . what parents do with their children is more important than who parents are.
>
> Sylva et al. (2004: v)

The EPPSE research shows the significance of quality home learning environments, where parents are involved in a process of 'active cultivation'. Children who were part of the study did better socially and intellectually when their Early Years settings shared educational aims and promoted high levels of parental involvement. Children's home literacy experiences were enriched when parents took part in activities similar to those in pre-school, such as reading stories, storytelling, mealtime conversations, games with numbers, painting and drawing, and visits to the library as well as taking children on outings and making time for them to play with friends at home (Sylva et al., 2004). Research has also shown that children who were perceived as clever developed a positive image of themselves as learners, and this was reinforced by family and by staff in the Early Years setting. High expectations were self-fulfilling (Siraj-Blatchford et al., 2011).

Quality pre-school settings

Pre-school settings that establish good relationships with parents can counter some of the disadvantages of the less successful home learning environments where parents perceive themselves as 'helpless' in their parenting. When literacy is seen as a skill that is first learnt in school, taught by professionals, parents can worry that they will do the 'wrong thing' if they try to help their children to learn to read and write. Parents can feel anxious and judged when their child is compared to others and when the focus is on the finished product of writing.

Early Years practitioners can reassure parents and help them to see that they can and do make a positive contribution towards their child's learning and development when they share ideas for everyday literacy activities, linked to children's preoccupations and interests. Enjoyable home learning experiences provide the fertile soil that help children to take more from high quality Early Years provision.

Bridging home and setting literacies

Liz Brooker's (2002) study of a group of children in a poor, ethnically diverse area of London describes the complex experiences of children, their parents and Early Years practitioners, when children start school and become 'pupils'.

Learning to be a pupil

One group of children in the study came from home environments where they experienced similar resources, activities and expectations to those that they met when they started school – children who had 'quality' home learning environments (Siraj-Blatchford et al., 2011). They discovered familiar resources and activities when they started school and, on the whole, they settled quickly and were seen by practitioners as ready for school learning. The children's experience of bedtime stories, songs and rhymes aligned their home culture with that of the Early Years setting. In contrast, children in the study who came from ethnic minority or 'marginalized' backgrounds found that they had to learn a new identity as pupils. Their home learning experiences were different from the culture of the setting, and positive experiences such as cooking alongside an adult or attendance at mosque school weren't acknowledged in activity planning. These children found it harder to access the curriculum and so they were perceived as not being ready for school learning. Children struggled to learn the expectations of the Early Years setting as they had to 'learn to be someone different altogether' (Brooker, 2002: 111).

Learning to be a parent of a school child

Parents' experiences of learning to fit into the school culture were as varied as their children's experiences. Brooker (2002) found that communication between Early Years practitioners and 'mainstream' parents was often comfortable and relaxed, made easier by a shared understanding of the educational aims of the setting. These parents understood what it meant to be a parent of a school child and they were able to support their child's learning.

However, communication was difficult or non-existent between staff and the parents whose own experiences of schooling had been difficult or very different from that of their child. These parents found it hard to help their children to access school learning effectively, even though they might have high aspirations. Parents who have experienced a formal, traditional education in their home country can experience a child-centred Early Years setting as undisciplined and chaotic and children are given mixed messages.

Being an inclusive practitioner

> No child should be expected to cast off the language and culture of home as he (sic) crosses the school threshold . . . The curriculum should reflect many elements of that part of his (sic) life which a child lives outside school.
>
> DES (1975: 286)

In previous chapters we have seen that, when project practitioners observed and supported children's learning styles and interests and listened to children's voices, children became motivated and confident learners. Practitioners became better at tuning in to the needs of boys and girls, and their observations helped them to recognize and value the experiences and strengths of children whose home culture was different from that of their Early Years setting. Instead of expecting children to become 'someone different altogether', practitioners found simple ways to adapt the setting to support the children.

Working with parents to support early writing

Some ways of reflecting diverse home literacy experiences in the setting

- Display print in different languages: put newspapers and magazines in a range of languages and scripts in the home corner and role play areas; use food packets from other countries for model making; write labels for displays in English and in children's home languages
- Make a library of song books and laminated sheets which children can take home to share with their family. Ask parents to share stories and songs from their own culture and to translate English songs and rhymes into their child's first language
- Involve parents in recording songs, rhymes and simple messages onto 'talking albums' and 'talking tins' in English and other home languages
- Create a set of core stories and help all children to become familiar with these by sending a copy of the stories home. Parents can read the book in their home language and in English
- Make personalized books with children, using photographs from the setting and from home. Scribe the child's words in English and in their home language

Figure 7.1 A 'talking album'

117

- Include resources that children see at home in the home corner. Be sensitive about how you introduce resources that might be unfamiliar to some children, to ensure that they are used appropriately.

> 'We made a beanstalk with giant leaves, climbing up Jason's bunkbed. We wrote a word on each leaf, a word that was important to him: family names, Tor (our dog), his favourite food (pickled onions and chicken!), his special toys and places we've been to on holiday. The beanstalk grew and grew and Jason grew more and more proud of himself as he recognized lots of the words!'

Developing a partnership with parents to support children's early writing

Almost without exception, parents want their children to do well educationally, but some parents are less confident than others at supporting their child and some parents believe that children only learn to read and write when they start school and are taught by trained professionals. There is evidence to show that interventions that help increase parents' confidence to support their child's learning have long-term benefits and are more effective than interventions that just work with children in school or in pre-school (Bronfenbrenner, 1974).

During the writing projects, practitioners shared information with parents about how young children become writers, through display boards, in workshops and by talking to parents informally. They stressed the value of activities that parents were already doing at home, and they gave parents some new ideas of simple, fun activities to do with their child. They shared stories about the children's learning journeys, activities and achievements and parents were encouraged to share children's learning stories from home. This helped parents to become more observant and 'tune in' to their children's early literacy behaviour. Parents reported a change in children's attitudes to mark making, drawing, reading and writing at home. One mother said she was 'thrilled with Jono's enthusiasm.' Another parent said her son is 'suddenly wanting to write,' while Frank 'writes more at home, he thinks school is fun and would like to invite his teacher home to play!'

Practitioners welcomed parents to take part in activities and events, helping them to see that children learn to write in relaxed and playful activities. One Reception class recognized that their children rarely took part in shared literacy activities at home with men, so they invited dads, older brothers, granddads and other male members of the children's families to come and make books and read with the children and to support their play. During the session, they made books about superheroes; they built rocket launchers and drew maps of planets, drawing craters, volcanoes and other landmarks; they read books together; they built dens and wrote signs.

A children's centre changed their entrance to create a comfortable, inviting reading area with attractively displayed, accessible books. This had the immediate impact of inspiring lots of parents and carers to share books with their child at the start and end of the session.

One of the project pre-schools made a display with information about the early stages of mark making, with photographs showing children making marks in gloop, finger paints, drinking chocolate, toothpaste, sand and compost – all of which children can do at home. They explained that children develop the fine motor skills needed for writing through these simple activities, and they can build a rich vocabulary and language that supports their thinking if an adult sits and talks with them as they play.

Practical and effective ways to increase communication between the setting and the home

- Have a whiteboard, chalkboard or large scrapbook where staff and parents can jot down daily news and comments from home and the setting
- Ask children and families to bring in photos or significant things from home, as a starting point for learning
- Hold workshops for parents on how children learn to write
- Create an information board for parents about how children learn to write and read, and the importance of play
- Give information to parents whose children are learning English as an additional language about the importance of keeping the child's first language going
- Hold a 'come and see how we learn to write' workshop for parents, and make writing packs

Working with parents to support early writing

- Photocopy and send home large speech bubbles, with the words: *Just to let you know at home I . . .*
- Create a board to display the speech bubbles when the child brings them back into the setting, and for children's independent writing from home
- Ask parents to make resources to support children's active learning, such as superhero capes (enough for every child) and story sack props
- Ask parents to contribute role play resources linked to their work, for example, plumbers' or carpenters' tools
- Ask parents to help put together lunchboxes or rucksacks for 'writing on the move'
- Invite dads, granddads and other male role models to come and get involved in literacy activities
- Encourage parents and carers to play 'I spy' on the way home, looking for environmental print.

> Patrick, age 4, brought in a story that he wrote at home with his older brother. He put it on the class display board, and this sparked off a flurry of independent writing by lots of other children, boys and girls.

Making open-ended writing packs to encourage writing at home

One nursery school developed a writing pack for all of the children to support the process of 'active cultivation' (Siraj-Blatchford *et al.*, 2011) of learning at home. Mark making and writing was encouraged by giving children a simple writing pack, a plastic wallet containing non-prescriptive mark making materials that encourage children to experiment with writing for many different purposes, freely and independently. The packs support early writing by sharing educational aims with parents, giving them information about how young children learn to write, and by valuing and encouraging parents' own contribution to children's learning. In this setting, they were given to children at home visits or when they made initial visits to the setting.

The writing packs were initially developed using the ORIM framework (Hannon, 1995) described in Chapter 5 to make links between learning at home and in the setting. The packs:

- gave children *opportunities* to write in their play: they help to motivate children to write by giving them a purpose for writing and the opportunity to practice in a relaxed, supportive environment
- helped parents to *recognize* when mark making is early writing and to *interact* to encourage their children to write
- encouraged parents to *model* writing alongside their children (Cigman, 1996).

Creating writing packs

Writing packs can contain a variety of open-ended mark making materials, such as:

- Envelopes
- White and coloured paper and card
- Stickers, labels, tags and Post-its
- Blank diaries and calendars
- Forms from the bank or post office
- Home-made books in different shapes and sizes
- Postcards
- Pencils, felt tips, crayons
- Paper clips
- Blu-tack.

> 'Felipe looked in the food cupboard and told me what we needed to buy. We wrote a shopping list together on some coloured paper from the writing pack – I wrote most of it, but Felipe made his own marks and he wrote all the "f"s. Then we found the things we needed in the supermarket, by matching up the words on our list and the words on the packets.'

A 'scrap box' was provided in the nursery containing similar mark making materials so the children could replenish the packs, and brief information was given to the parents about how to use the packs.

Working with parents to support early writing

Using the writing pack – for parents

- Remember that the pack belongs to your child. Keep it somewhere accessible
- Focus on writing for a real reason – write a shopping list or make a birthday card. Don't ask your child to copy letter shapes
- Let your child choose when and how to use the pack
- You can make suggestions and share ideas for activities, but the pack isn't intended to be 'homework' so don't put pressure on your child to use it
- Don't . . . criticize – children need to write in their play just like they play cooking or mending things
- Don't . . . worry! Your child will develop confidence and learn by experimenting and playing
- Do . . . encourage, praise and support
- Do . . . have fun together!

> Louis wrote in his holiday diary: *Whace up from sleeping. Mia came to play. Go to bed.*

Suggestions of things to do with the writing pack

- Create an office space. It doesn't have to be large and it doesn't have to cost anything. Collect old envelopes, forms, diaries, calendars; make books by stapling different sized scraps of paper together; collect a variety of pens, pencils, crayons
- Write messages to your child, and respond to your child's written messages even if you can't 'read' them. Ask your child to read the message to you
- Write a menu for meal times
- Write stories with your child. Encourage them to make up their own stories about their pictures, friends or outings. You can be their 'secretary' until they can write for themselves, but encourage them to have a go if they want to
- Talk about words, signs and numbers in the street and around the house
- Cut pictures out of toy catalogues and make a scrapbook of your child's favourite toys
- Write special events on a calendar: birthdays, outings, visits to the doctor.

Working with parents to support early writing

In one project setting, parents made writing packs at a workshop together. The teacher reported very positive feedback from the parents who felt more confident in their ability to support their child's early mark making, and they enjoyed having new ideas and resources.

> 'Shoaib wrote "instruction manuals" for all of his cars in the little books from his writing pack.'

Conclusion

During the first few years of life, parents see their child go through an astonishing learning journey, at the child's own pace, at home, without any formal teaching or assessments. During the boys' writing projects, practitioners aimed to build on the fertile soil of the home environment to continue this learning journey. They responded to each child as an individual, taking account of their age, their developmental stage and their varying experiences so far, to create learning opportunities that would allow every child to become a confident member of the 'literacy club' (Smith, 1988), with their own unique voice.

Summary: Helping boys to become motivated writers by creating a partnership with parents

The project has helped with the challenge of getting parents on board, who have more formal expectations.

- Acknowledge that all parents are keen to support their child's early literacy development, and let every parent know that you value their individual role as their child's first educator
- Acknowledge and support the diversity of home literacy experiences
- Share the educational aims of the literacy activities that take place in the setting
- Help parents to feel confident in letting children experiment with writing and 'have a go'

123

Working with parents to support early writing

- Suggest new ideas and resources that will help all parents to create 'fertile soil' for children's literacy development and support writing at home
- Create spaces where children's independent writing from home and in the setting can be displayed and shared, to create a dialogue among and between parents, children and practitioners.

8 Conclusion

Frank is now a true writer. He is confident in his own abilities and takes real pride in whatever he produces. This project has helped to empower him and take away the pressure that was holding him back. He has a natural ability that blossomed under the conditions we developed.

Frank is just one of the many boys who benefited from the boys' writing projects: boys who became more confident and competent writers, and who also became more confident and competent children. So how does this picture of Frank fit with the comment by a colleague who, when he heard that I was writing a book about boys' writing in the Early Years, asked: *'Do you mean troublesome boys or all boys? Well, I suppose all boys are troublesome.'*

Boys often see negative images of themselves and their male role models in the media, where they are presented as 'little rascals and tearaways' who will become teenage hoodies, thugs and yobs (*Women in Journalism*, 2009) who will have a midlife crisis involving fast cars or motorbikes, before they settle down into 'grumpy old men'. Boys' T-shirts set up expectations with slogans such as *'Watch out! Trouble's arrived'*, *'Be thankful I'm not your kid'* and *'I can shout REALLY, REALLY LOUD.'*

These images are sometimes subtle and always powerful, and they influence all of us, male and female. Research conducted by the University of Kent showed that gender stereotypes are formed at a very young age, and that stereotypes affect children's expectations of how well boys and girls will achieve in school. Boys and girls who took part in the study expected boys to do less well than girls academically. However, the research also provided a positive message, that 'it is possible to improve boys' performance . . . by

Conclusion

conveying egalitarian messages' (Society for Research in Child Development, 2013).

Redefining our image and expectations of boys

> ### A troublesome boy or a confident, logical thinker?
>
> A father of two boys told the following story:
>
> *'I was bringing the kids back from a cinema trip. Benjie and Zach were noisy and busy with endless variations of poo jokes and stories, just enjoying playing around with the word. I commented that I don't think passengers on the bus like hearing the word "poo".*
>
> *Benjie immediately replied that he's a passenger on the bus and he likes hearing the word.'*

It is the contention of this book that the image of boys as generally 'troublesome' is inaccurate and damaging. In an education system that prioritizes the transmission of knowledge over the development of learning skills, young boys' active, often boisterous style of learning can be inconvenient and sometimes problematic in group settings. Boys commonly challenge conventional expectations of behaviour (as Benjie did); they can find it harder than girls to sit and listen and process instructions; they can find it harder to follow an external agenda.

However, in a creative, flexible educational system that values intrinsic motivation, challenge, active learning and investigation, boys (and girls) thrive. In this context, we can redefine 'troublesome' boys as curious and inquisitive, who enjoy problem-seeking and problem-solving. During the boys' writing projects, practitioners countered the negative stereotyping of young boys by responding positively to their styles of behaviour and play. They looked for ways to create an environment that conveyed 'egalitarian messages', where boys and girls felt equally comfortable, and all children were able to develop their confidence as learners.

Improving boys' confidence, motivation and attainment as writers

The examples of good practice described in each chapter of this book show that the boys' writing projects worked on two levels. First, they focused on *writing* as a communicative tool, emphasizing compositional skills over transcriptional skills. Practitioners recognized that writing is an expressive art as well as having a functional purpose; that writing is a cognitive tool that supports abstract thinking and it is a social tool that helps children relate to each other. So project practitioners supported children's holistic development as they transformed their learning environments into writing workshops.

Second, the projects focused on *boys* and this allowed practitioners to provide spaces and resources where boys could follow their interests and take initiative in their learning. Practitioners created learning environments that were more suited to active learning, appropriate to young children's developmental needs, and so all children benefited.

A child-centred pedagogy for boys and girls

In 2011, a national project asked children what they thought would make the perfect school and the many inspired ideas that they came up with were collated into the Children's Manifesto. Boys and girls showed that they understood the impact of the physical environment on learning, by suggesting that schools should have playgrounds that presented challenges such as rock climbing and places where they could learn about nature. They asked for comfortable spaces with beanbags, 'a pink fluffy carpet' and a chill-out room. They understood that learning can't be rushed, requesting time to finish 'something that needs a lot of thinking'. They asked for inclusive and international schools. Some of the big ideas were clearly impractical, such as having Gordon Ramsay to cook their dinners and Stephen Hawking to teach science, but their reasoning was sound: teachers should be experts and people who are passionate about their subject. (http://www.theguardian.com/education/2011/may/03/school-i-would-like-childrens-manifesto?CMP=twt_gu)

What would a manifesto for boys include, if we consider the type of setting that boys would like? Toy and computer game manufacturers know very well

Conclusion

how to appeal to boys and they use their knowledge effectively to sell their products. The challenge to all Early Years practitioners is to be just as good at appealing to boys, so that we can support their learning.

Inspired by the Children's Manifesto and the work of boys' writing projects, here are some suggestions for a Boys' Manifesto:

A Boys' Manifesto – the Early Years setting we'd like

Being active

We would like places and spaces where we can run . . . jump . . . climb . . . dig . . . hide

Places where we can kick and throw a ball

Places where we can fire an arrow from a bow, weave a giant web or launch a rocket into space

Being still

We need quiet spaces

Mats and beanbags where we can sit and read

Places where we can lie down, stretch out and draw or write or think

Messy play with natural materials

We love playing with water, sand, mud, twigs, bark, clay

Real-life experiences

We would like to keep animals, have a wormery, build a bird hide

We're interested in people who can tell us about their work: builders, firefighters, librarians, bus drivers, farmers

We love real-life problems to solve: building a tall tower, making a bridge that can carry a car across some guttering, making up some music for a superhero celebration

Conclusion

Creative and imaginative play

We like to stretch our imaginations by being superheroes, flying to the moon, going on adventures on magic carpets and chasing dragons

We like to pretend to be people who inspire us, like our dads or our heroes in books and on television and computer games

We like to make up jokes and be a little bit mischievous!

Time to follow through fascinations

We need time to explore new ideas and places

. . . time to find out new facts

. . . time to experiment, to see what works and to find out how to improve the things that don't work

Adults to help

We need adults who listen to every one of us

. . . adults who help us to problem seek and problem solve

. . . adults who find resources to improve our play

. . . adults who write down our ideas and stories and who help us to write for ourselves

. . . adults who care for everyone

. . . adults who explain what we need to do to fit in and who let us do our own thing sometimes

. . . adults who read to us, and who inspire and make learning irresistible

. . . adults who give us time to concentrate on play that is important to us

Conclusion

Final words

All adults have backed off the treadmill of getting children through activities and are spending more time listening to children

During the writing projects, practitioners discovered and responded to the voices reflected in the Boys' Manifesto, spending quality time alongside children, working respectfully together. Practitioners established safe boundaries that helped boys to feel secure and able to explore and take risks in their learning, and they appealed to the boys' innate curiosity, playfulness and resourcefulness as learners. The boys responded with energy, creativity and enjoyment as they discovered that writing could enhance their understanding of the world and their place in the world.

Establishing a child-centred pedagogy also helped the girls, as boys and girls played alongside each other and inspired each other to write. If we want children to continue to be playful and inventive thinkers and writers we need to listen to, and take inspiration from their stories.

Appendix 1
Boys' Writing Project – the action planning process

1. Starting the project – audit and observations

- **What are the current strengths** in your setting's provision for speaking, listening, mark making, drawing and writing?
- **Opportunities in the continuous provision**: what opportunities are available to boys inside and out? Are mark making resources attractively presented and freely available? Can they be used flexibly? Is there a good range of choice?
- **Observing children's play and learning**: do children independently and confidently choose to explore their ideas through mark making? What are the boys' interests and learning styles? Where are they choosing to go and what are they choosing to do?
- **Support from adults**: is mark making valued by all practitioners in the setting? How do they plan, model, support, encourage and extend these experiences?

2. Making the changes

- What changes have you decided to implement?
- How will you work with your colleagues to put the changes into practice?
- What impact do you hope that these changes will have?
- What resources will you need? What is the time frame?
- How will you involve the children and their parents in this process?
- How will you know if the changes have improved the quality of provision?

Appendix 1

3. Evaluating the impact of changes

- What evidence do you have of the ways in which children are now engaging in freely chosen mark making experiences – for example, ongoing observations, photographs and examples of children's 'work'?
- Have the changes succeeded in improving the quality of provision? How do you know? If not, why not?
- What has made the biggest difference?
- How has this benefited the children?
- What might you have done differently?

4. What next?

- How will you carry this work forward? What will your next focus be? For example, will you continue to develop provision; continue to develop classroom practice; develop staff training; develop transitions from the previous setting and into the next?

Adapted from a document by Sally Jaeckle

Appendix 2
Boys' Writing Project play audit

Resources to support boys' writing inside and outside

By the end of the EYFS . . . (Taken from: DFE and Standards and Testing Agency, 2013)	Enabling environment – some opportunities for communication, language, mark making and writing	What do we have now?	What do we need?
Communication and Language **ELG 01 Listening and attention:** Children listen attentively in a range of situations. They listen to stories, accurately anticipating key events, and respond to what they hear with relevant comments, questions or actions. They give their attention to what others say and respond appropriately, while engaged in another activity.	**Water and . . .** – boats – sea creatures – shells and pebbles – ice – bubbles **Wet and dry sand and . . .** – sea creatures – natural materials – cars – moulds – small containers and spoons **Investigation table** – magnifying glasses, bug boxes		

Appendix 2

By the end of the EYFS . . . (Taken from: DFE and Standards and Testing Agency, 2013)	Enabling environment – some opportunities for communication, language, mark making and writing	What do we have now?	What do we need?
ELG 02 Understanding: Children follow instructions involving several ideas or actions. They answer 'how' and 'why' questions about their experiences and in response to stories or events. **ELG 03 Speaking:** Children express themselves effectively, showing awareness of listeners' needs. They use past, present and future forms accurately when talking about events that have happened or are to happen in the future. They develop their own narratives and explanations by connecting ideas or events.	**Cooking** **Sensory/tactile experiences (with interesting things added)** – cornflour (Gloop) – playdough – mud kitchens – clay – rice – gravel – treasure baskets **Woodwork** **Workshop** **Books** **Construction** **Role play with dressing-up clothes** **Small world** – minibeasts – dinosaurs – sea creatures – farm animals – cars/vehicles – boats **Puppets** **Musical instruments**		

Appendix 2

By the end of the EYFS . . . (Taken from: DFE and Standards and Testing Agency, 2013)	Enabling environment – some opportunities for communication, language, mark making and writing	What do we have now?	What do we need?
	Tapes/CDs – music from different countries/cultures – songs **Resources for movement** – ribbons – lightweight fabric **Puzzles and games** **Walks/outings** **ICT** – Roamer – tape recorder		
Literacy development involves encouraging children to read and write, both through listening to others reading, and being encouraged to begin to read and write themselves. Children must be given access to a wider range of reading materials – books, poems, and other written materials, to ignite their interest.	**A print-rich environment** – labels – signs – displays with children's stories and comments scribed **Fiction books** – in dens – in role play – home-made **Information books** – in all areas **CDs with fiction books and songs and rhymes** **Puppets** **Storyboards and story sacks**		

135

Appendix 2

By the end of the EYFS ... (Taken from: DFE and Standards and Testing Agency, 2013)	Enabling environment – some opportunities for communication, language, mark making and writing	What do we have now?	What do we need?
ELG 10 Writing: Children use their phonic knowledge to write words in ways which match their spoken sounds. They also write some irregular common words. They write sentences which can be read by themselves and others. Some words are spelt correctly and others are phonetically plausible.	**A well-equipped writing area** – different size and shape home-made books – a range of writing materials – clipboards – home-made books – children's own display boards – whiteboards – sticky labels, Blu-tack and card **Writing resources accessible everywhere Places to write and mark make on a large scale** – on the floor – on walls **An inviting book area** – poems, rhymes and rhyming language – with repetitive language – home-made books **Games** – sound/letter – rhyming **Computer/interactive whiteboard** **Magnetic letters and boards**		

Appendix 2

By the end of the EYFS... (Taken from: DFE and Standards and Testing Agency, 2013)	Enabling environment – some opportunities for communication, language, mark making and writing	What do we have now?	What do we need?
	Cooking – recipe books and cards – photograph books – packets and labels **Writing 'on the move'** – writing resources in rucksacks, buckets, belts, bags . . . – clipboards – whiteboards/blackboards – plans and maps **Role play** – writing frames – notebooks **Small and large construction** – labels – writing about models **Investigation** Clipboards		
Physical Development involves providing opportunities for young children to be active and interactive, and to develop their coordination, control, and movement **ELG 04 Moving and handling:** They handle equipment and tools effectively, including pencils for writing.	**Large play equipment for gross motor development** **Woodwork** **Workshop** **Construction** **Computer** **Wet and dry sand**		

137

Appendix 2

By the end of the EYFS... (Taken from: DFE and Standards and Testing Agency, 2013)	Enabling environment – some opportunities for communication, language, mark making and writing	What do we have now?	What do we need?
	Paint – different size brushes and sponges **Clay** – and tools **Water** – different size brushes – washing up liquid bottles – sprays		

Appendix 3
Boys' Writing Project case study

Name _____ D.O.B. _____

A description of (name) in (date)	Encouraging and inspiring: What changes did we make?	Observations: What did we observe along the way?	A description of (name) in (date)

Appendix 4
Boys' Writing Project – end of project summary

How can we improve boys' confidence, motivation and attainment as writers?

Name of school/setting: _____

Name of lead practitioner: _____

Context of school/setting _____
(size of EYFS, catchment):

1. Starting the project: What did we learn from the initial audit, tracking and observations?

2. What did we decide to change? Writing an action plan

Appendix 4

3. Evaluating the changes: significant developments, showing the impact on boys' confidence, motivation and attainment as writers (this might be individual children or the whole class)

4. What next?

References and further reading

Anning, A. and Ring, K. (2004) *Making Sense of Children's Drawings* Maidenhead: Open University Press.

Auerbach, E.R. (1989) 'Towards a Socio-Contextual Approach to Family Literacy.' *Harvard Educational Review* 59(2): 165–81.

Baron-Cohen, S. (2004) *The Essential Difference: Men, Women and the Extreme Male Brain*. London: Penguin.

Bertram, A.D. (1996) 'Effective Early Childhood Educators: Developing a Methodology for Improvement, Volume 1'. Unpublished PhD thesis, Coventry University.

Bissex, G. (1980) *Gnys at Wrk*. Cambridge, MA: Harvard University Press.

Brault, R. (n.d.) *A Robert Brault Reader* blog. www.robertbrault.com (accessed 8 August 2013).

Bromley, H. (2006) *Making My Own Mark: Play and Writing*. London: The British Association for Early Childhood Education.

Bronfenbrenner, U. (1974) *A Report on Longitudinal Evaluations of Preschool Programs, Vol. 2, Is Early Intervention Effective?* Washington, DC: DHEW, Publication No. (OHD), 74-25.

Brooker, L. (2002) *Starting School: Young Children Learning Cultures*. Buckingham: Open University Press.

Bruce, T. (1997) *Early Childhood Education*. London: Hodder & Stoughton.

Bruner, J.S. (1977) *The Process of Education*. London: Harvard University Press.

Cigman, J. (1996) 'Creating Links between Home and School Literacies: Working with Parents to Develop and Evaluate a Literacy Pack for Children Starting at Nursery.' Unpublished M.Ed. thesis: University of Sheffield School of Education.

Clark, A. and Moss, P. (2011) *Listening to Young Children: The Mosaic Approach*. London: NCB.

Claxton, G. (2005) *Building Learning Power*. Bristol: TLO.

Claxton, G. (2008) *What's the Point of School?* Oxford: Oneworld Publications.

Corbett, P. (2010) *How to Teach Story Writing at Key Stage 1*. Abingdon: David Fulton Publishers.

Csikszentmihalyi, M. (2002) *Flow: The Psychology of Happiness*. London: Rider.

David, T. (1999) *Changing Minds: Teaching Young Children*. In David, T. (ed.) *Teaching Young Children* London: Paul Chapman Publishing, pp. 1–18.

DCSF (2009) *Gender and Education – Mythbusters Addressing Gender and Achievement: Myths and Realities*. London: DCSF Publications.

de Boo, M. (ed.) (2004) *Early Years Handbook*. Sheffield: Curriculum Partnership.

DES (1975) *The Bullock Report A Language for Life*. London: Her Majesty's Stationery Office.

Dewey, John (1897) 'My Pedagogic Creed.' *The School Journal* LIV(3) (January 16): 77–80. http://infed.org/mobi/john-dewey-my-pedagogical-creed/ (accessed February 9 2013).

DFE (2012) *Statutory Framework for the Early Years Foundation Stage*. London: DFE.

DFE and Standards and Testing Agency (2013) *Early Years Foundation Stage Profile: Handbook 2014*. https://www.gov.uk/government/publications/early-years-foundation-stage-profile-handbook-2014 (accessed 16 October 2013).

Duffy, B. (1998) *Supporting Creativity and Imagination in the Early Years*. Buckingham: Open University Press.

Early Education (2012) *Development Matters in the Early Years Foundation Stage (EYFS)*. http://www.early-education.org.uk/publications-and-resources/1435 (accessed 5 January 2013).

Edwards, C., Gandini, L. and Forman, G. (eds) (1998) *'The Hundred Languages of Children': The Reggio Emilia Approach – Advanced Reflections*. Norwood, NJ: Ablex Publishing.

Ferreiro, E. and Teberosky, A. (1982) *Literacy before Schooling*. New York: Heinemann Educational Books.

Fisher, J. (1996) *Starting from the Child?* Buckingham: Open University Press.

Fisher, K., Hirsh-Pasek, K., Golinkoff, R.M., Singer, D.G. and Berk, L. (2011) *Playing Around in School: Implications for Learning and Educational Policy*.

References and further reading

In Pellegrini, A. (ed.) *The Oxford Handbook of the Development of Play*. New York: Oxford University Press, pp. 341–62.

Goddard Blythe, S. (2005) *The Well Balanced Child*. Stroud: Hawthorn Press.

Goodman, Y. (1986) 'Children Coming to Know Literacy.' In Teale, William and Sulzby, E. (eds) *Emergent Literacy*. Norwood, NJ: Ablex, pp. 1–14.

Gopnik, A. (2009) *The Philosophical Baby*. London: The Bodley Head.

Gussin Paley, V. (1986) *Boys and Girls – Superheroes in the Doll Corner*. Chicago, IL: The University of Chicago Press.

Gussin Paley, V. (2004) *A Child's Work*. http://www.press.uchicago.edu/Misc/Chicago/644871.html (accessed 9 August 2013).

Gussin Paley, V. (2008) Vivian Gussin Paley at 92Y Wonderplay Conference 2008. http://www.youtube.com/watch?v=wWxYRkmHNXM (accessed 17 September 2013).

Hall, N. and Robinson, A. (2003) *Exploring Writing and Play in the Early Years*. London: David Fulton Publishers.

Hannon, P. (1992) *Preschool Intervention in Literacy Development: Some British Research*. In Fase, W., Kreft, W., Leseman, P. and Slavenburg, J. (eds) *Illiteracy in the European Community: Research Problems and Research Findings*. De Lier: Academisch Boeken Centrum, pp. 123–37.

Hannon, P. (1995) *Literacy, Home and School*. London: Falmer Press.

Holland, P. (2002) 'War, Weapon and Superhero Play: A Challenge to Zero Tolerance.' Summary of paper presented at 4th Warwick International Early Years Conference, Warwick, March 2002.

Katz, L. (2011) 'Current Perspectives on the Early Childhood Curriculum.' In House, R. (ed.) *Too Much, Too Soon?* Stroud: Hawthorn Press, pp. 118–30.

Laevers, F. (ed.) (2005) *Sics (Ziko) Well-being and Involvement in Care Settings: A Process-oriented Self-evaluation Instrument*. Leuven: Kind & Gezin and Research Centre for Experiential Education.

Leach, P. (2011) 'The EYFS and the Real Foundations of Children's Early Years.' In House, R. (ed.) *Too Much, Too Soon?* Stroud: Hawthorn Press, pp. 21–35.

MacLure, M. and Jones, L. (2009) *Classroom Behaviour: Why It's Hard to Be Good*. http://www.esrc.ac.uk/news-and-events/press-releases/2821/Classroom_behaviour_why_its_hard_to_be_good_.aspx (accessed 7 August 2013).

Malaguzzi, Loris. n.d. *Reggio-Inspired*. http://reggioinspired.ning.com/forum/topics/loris-malaguzzi (accessed 4 August 2013).

Miller, E. and Almon, J. (2009) *Crisis in the Kindergarten: Why Children Need to Play in School*. College Park, MD: Alliance for Childhood.

Nutbrown, Cathy (1994) *Threads of Thinking*. London: Paul Chapman Publishing.
Podmore, Valerie N. and Luff, Paulette (2012) *Observation: Origins and Approaches*. Maidenhead: Open University Press.
Pound, L and Harrison, C. (2003) *Supporting Musical Development in the Early Years*. Maidenhead: Open University Press.
Primary National Strategy (2007) *Confident, Capable and Creative: Supporting Boys' Achievements*. London: DCSF Publications.
Rinaldi, C. (2006) *In Dialogue with Reggio Emilia*. Abingdon: Routledge.
Rose, J. and Rogers, S. (2012) *The Role of the Adult in Early Years Settings*. Maidenhead: Open University Press.
Siraj-Blatchford, I., Mayo, A., Melhuish, E., Taggart, B., Sammons, P. and Sylva, K. (2011) *Performing against the Odds: Developmental Trajectories of Children in the EPPSE 3-16 Study*. Institute of Education, University of London, Birkbeck, University of London, University of Oxford
Smith, F. (1988) *Joining the Literacy Club*. Portsmouth, NH: Heinemann Educational.
Society for Research in Child Development (2013) Press Release: *Negative Stereotypes about Boys Hinder their Academic Development*. http://www.labspaces.net/126754/Negative_stereotypes_about_boys_hinder_their_academic_achievement (accessed 19 July 2013).
Sylva, K., Melhuish, E.C., Sammons, P., Siraj-Blatchford, I. and Taggart, B. (2004) *Technical Paper 12 The Final Report: Effective Pre-School Education*. London: Institute of Education University of London.
Taylor, D. (1983) *Family Literacy*. Exeter, NH: Heinemann Educational.
The National Strategies Early Years (2008) *Mark Making Matters*. London: DCSF Publications.
The National Writing Project (1989) *Becoming a Writer*. Walton on Thames: Thomas Nelson & Sons.
Thornton, L. and Brunton, P. (2007) *Bringing the Reggio Approach to Your Early Years Practice*. Abingdon: David Fulton Publishers.
Tickell, C. (2011) *The Early Years: Foundations for Life, Health and Learning*. https://www.gov.uk/government/publications/the-early-years-foundations-for-life-health-and-learning-an-independent-report-on-the-early-years-foundation-stage-to-her-majestys-government (accessed 1 March 2013).
Vygotsky, L.S. (1962) *Thought and Language*. Cambridge, MA: MIT Press.
Vygotsky, L.S. (1978) *Mind in Society: The Development of Higher Psychological Processes*. Cambridge, MA: Harvard University Press.

Whitehead, Marion R. (2004) *Language and Literacy in the Early Years*. London: Sage Publications.
Women in Journalism (2009) 'Hoodies or Altar Boys: What Is Media Stereotyping Doing to Our British Boys?' *Women in Journalism*. http://womeninjournalism.co.uk/hoodies-or-altar-boys/ (accessed 12 April 2012).

Index

action planning xiii,131
adult-led learning xxi, 95
adventure themes 48
Almon, J. 14
assessment 44, 57, 76;
   observation-led i, xix, xxii;
   standardized xix, 16
attainment, raising xxv, 90,
attitudes to learning 1, 9, 37, 98, 118
audits xxiii, 16, 21, 22
author: becoming an 64, 65;
   area 46, 89, 98

Baron-Cohen, S. 42, 43, 79, 101
behaviour 37, 39, 41, 102, 126; and gender differences 43
Berk, L. 22, 77
Bissex, G. 60, 62
boundaries 42, 79, 95;
   consistent 78; safe 130
brain types: systemizing brain 43;
   empathizing brain 43, 79
Brault, R. 16
Bronfenbrenner, U. 118
Brooker, L. 115, 116
Bruce, T. 58, 59
Bruner, J. 63, 64, 75, 113

case studies xxiii
characteristics of effective learning (EYFS) 20
child-initiated learning xxi, 22, 82, 84, 94, 95
child involvement *see* wellbeing and involvement
choice 23, 76; boards 99
Cigman, J. 121
classroom research xxii
classroom as 'third educator' 20
Claxton, G. xxi, 37, 57, 63
communication and language 50, 96, 100, 101, 133–38
compositional writing skills 2, 4, 9, 10, 54, 92, 127
confidence xxi, 9, 36, 93, 97, 111, 122, 126, 127
construction and model making 33, 110, 117
Corbett, P. 100
creativity xix, 38, 49, 110, 111, 130
Csikszentmihalyi, M. 19
curriculum 9, 78, 93, 94, 96, 115, 116; offered and received 95, 111; spiral 63; making connections across 94; *see also* Early Years Foundation Stage

Index

David, T. 110
dens 29, 51, 105, 106, 119; reading 32
developmental stages in writing xxiv, 2, 4, 9
Dewey, J. 75, 76
displays 22, 25, 26–7, 35, 45; bilingual 117; for parents 118, 120, 124

Early Years Foundation Stage (EYFS): communication and language 50, 96, 100, 101, 133–38; expressive arts and design 96, 108, 110; mathematics 96, 104, 111; personal, social and emotional development 91, 97, 98; physical development 96, 102; understanding the world 105–8 see also prime areas of learning; specific areas of learning
Edwards, C. 78, 93, 108
emotional development 20, 91, 97, 98
enabling environments xxi, 20, 35, 77, 92, 127, 128; evaluating 18, 21–2
EPPSE / EPPE 114
exploration 59, 60, 76
expressive arts and design 96, 108, 110

Ferreiro, E. 55
fine motor skills 15, 27, 33, 40, 90, 103, 111, 119
Fisher, J. 78, 95
Fisher, K. 22, 77
flow, state of 19
following children's interests 48, 64, 70, 94, 104, 111
Forman, G. 78, 93, 108

Gandini, L. 78, 93, 108
Goddard Blythe, S. 23, 39, 102

Golinkoff, R.M. 22, 77
Goodman, Y. 111, 112, 113
Gopnik, A. 94
gross motor skills 15, 27, 35, 90, 103, 111
Gussin Paley, V. xix, 39, 42, 51, 78

handwriting 2, 57, 74, 90, 103
Hannon, P. 74, 81, 120
Harrison, C. 23
Hirsh-Pasek, K. 22, 77
Holland, P. 40
home learning environment xxv, 113, 114, 115, 120, 123
hundred languages 93, 108, 109

inner speech 3

Jones, L. 41

Katz, L. 9, 78

Laevers, F. 19, 20, 53, 62, 94
learning dispositions 14, 37, 53, 74, 97, 110
learning targets 37, 38, 91
listening to children 35, 53, 92, 130
'literacy club' 1, 4, 7, 25, 36, 123
literacy: functional 111, 112; home 4, 111–13, 115, 117–20, 123–4; iceberg 81, 91; roots of 111, 112, 113 see also Goodman, Y.
Luff, P. 78

MacLure, M. 41
Malaguzzi, L. 74, 108
maps 43, 48, 69, 70, 98, 104, 105
mastery disposition 14, 37, 53
mathematics 96, 104, 111
Mayo, A. 112, 114, 115, 120
Melhuish, E. 112, 114, 115, 120
Miller, E. 14
modelling: writing 5, 16, 58, 68, 77, 88–9, 92; language 50, 60

motivation 9, 36–8, 58, 90, 97, 102, 126, 127; intrinsic 37, 126
movement 23, 90, 102
music 23, 28, 29, 71, 110, 128

National Writing Project 113
negotiated classroom 74, 77–8
New Zealand 110
numbers 5, 70, 93, 104, 114, 122
Nutbrown, C. 79

observations: use of xxii, 16, 75, 116; planning from 25, 86, 106
Ofsted xxii
oral language 2, 20, 24, 35; and writing 4, 50, 60, 70, 82, 100, 101, 113; resources for 24
ORIM model 74, 81, 120
outdoor learning xxi, 29, 39, 66

parents 37, 81, 112, 114–24
Persona Dolls 99
personal, social and emotional development 91, 97, 98
Piaget, J. 75, 93
phonics xxiv, 7, 9, 21, 37, 61, 64, 90
physical development 96, 102
planning, xxii, 38, 40, 53, 86, 91, 95, 115; with children 38, 47, 54, 68, 69, 99
play: active and physical 21, 39, 40–2, 48, 80, 84; as a mechanism for learning xxi, xxiii, 9, 14, 38, 78, 93–4; free flow 58, 59, 78, 82, 89, 111; environment 22, 23, 25, 77; stages of 59–60
plural practitioner 76
Podmore, V.N. 78
Pound, L. 23
prime areas of learning (EYFS) 97–103
private speech 3

Reggio Emilia 95
Rinaldi, C. 18, 20
role of the adult in supporting writing 74, 81, 91
role play 3, 21, 25, 29, 51, 68–9, 88, 104; areas 25, 117
Rogers, S. 76, 77, 95
Rose, J. 76, 77, 95
rough housing 42
routines 32, 39, 75, 82, 110

Sammons, P. 112, 114, 115, 120
scaffolding 72, 75, 77
scribing 4, 11, 49, 50, 73, 92
sensory materials 33

Singer, D.G. 22, 77

Siraj-Blatchford, I. 112, 114, 115, 120

Smith, F. 1, 36, 75, 123
social constructivist approach 75
specific areas of learning (EYFS) 104–110
spelling 4, 57, 58, 90; conventions 2, 9, 68, 96; independent 62; invented 62
story language 8, 100
storytelling 51, 66, 100, 114
superheroes 49, 64, 70, 80, 106, 119
Sylva, K. 112, 114, 115, 120

Taggart, B. 112, 114, 115, 120
targets see learning targets
Taylor, D. 24
Teberosky, A. 55
technology 96, 97, 107
testosterone 41
Te Whariki 110
Tickell, C. 37, 98
transcriptional writing skills 2, 4, 9, 16, 54, 57, 89–90, 92

Index

understanding the world 105–8

vestibular system 102
Vygotsky, L. 3, 63, 72, 75, 93

wellbeing and involvement: scales 19, 20; levels 28, 53, 62, 94
Whitehead, M. 55, 57, 60, 81
Women in Journalism 125
writing: area 22, 25, 26, 27, 35; as a symbolic system 4, 5, 90, 92; collaborative 26, 64, 86, 97; developmental stages 4–8, 9,17; independent 45, 62–3, 89, 92, 98, 120, 124; on a large scale 27, 28; 'on the move' 31, 120; packs 119–21, 123; for a purpose 25, 29, 55, 70, 72, 88, 90; *see also* compositional writing skills; transcriptional writing skills

zone of proximal development (ZPD) 63, 72, 75